THE
WILD
BOY

ALSO BY PAOLO COGNETTI

The Eight Mountains

THE WILD BOY

— *A Memoir* —

Paolo Cognetti

Translated by
Erica Segre and Simon Carnell

ATRIA PAPERBACK

New York   London   Toronto   Sydney   New Delhi

ATRIA
PAPERBACK

An Imprint of Simon & Schuster, Inc.
1230 Avenue of the Americas
New York, NY 10020

This book is for Gabriele and Remigio,
my mountain guides.

And to the memory of Chris McCandless,
guiding spirit.

I dwelt in the high day that lives
beyond the firs,
I walked in fields and on mountains
of light—
Crossed dead lakes—and a secret
song was whispered through
landlocked waves—
I crossed white shores, calling
by name
somnolent gentians—
I dreamt in the snow
an immense sunken city
of flowers—
I dwelt on the mountains
like an upstanding flower—
and looked at the rocks,
the other promontories
through the sea of winds—
and sang to myself of a remote
summer, that with its bitter
rhododendrons
burnt in my blood

Antonia Pozzi, "Snowfields"

WINTER

Season of Sleep

In the City

A few years back I had a difficult winter. It hardly seems important now to recall the reason for my malaise. I was thirty years old and felt drained, disoriented, and disillusioned, as you do when a project in which you believed ends miserably. Imagining the future at that moment seemed as unlikely as setting out on a voyage when you're sick and it's raining outside. I had tried hard, but what did I have to show for it? I was dividing my time between bookshops, hardware stores, the café bar in front of my house, and my bed, contemplating through a window the white sky of Milan. Above all, I was not writing, which for me is like not sleeping or not eating. I was in a kind of void that I'd never experienced before.

In those months, novels turned away from me, but I was attracted to stories of individuals who, rejecting the world, had sought solitude in the woods. I read Henry David Thoreau's *Walden* and *The History of a Mountain* by Élisée Reclus.

I was particularly taken by the journey of Chris McCandless as told by Jon Krakauer in *Into the Wild*. Perhaps because McCandless was not a nineteenth-century philosopher but a young man of my own time, who at the age of twenty-two had left the city, his family, his studies, a brilliant future as defined by the norms of Western society—and had set off on a solitary journey that would end with death by starvation in Alaska. When the story came to public attention he was judged by many to have made an idealistic choice amounting to a flight from reality, if not altogether to a suicidal impulse. I felt as if I understood it—and inwardly I admired it. Chris did not get the chance to write a book, perhaps he never even intended to do so, but he loved Thoreau and had adopted his manifesto:

I went to the woods because I wished to live deliberately, to front only the essential facts of life, and see if I could not learn what it had to teach, and not, when I came to die, discover that I had not lived. I did not wish to live what was not life, living is so dear; nor did I wish to practise resignation, unless it was quite necessary. I wanted to live deep and suck out all the marrow of life, to live so sturdily and Spartan-like as to put to rout all that was not life, to cut a broad swath and shave close, to drive life into a corner, and reduce it to its lowest terms, and, if it proved

to be mean, why then to get the whole and genuine meanness of it, and publish its meanness to the world; or if it
were sublime, to know it by experience, and be able to
give a true account of it in my next excursion.

I had not been back to the mountains for ten years. Until
I was twenty I had spent all my summers there. As a child
of the city, raised in an apartment, having grown up in a
neighborhood where it was not possible to go down into a
courtyard or out onto the street, the mountains for me had
represented an idea of absolute liberty. Brutally at first, and
then very naturally, I had learned how to navigate up there
just as other children learn to swim because an adult flung
them into water: at eight or nine I had started to tread the
glaciers and get my hands on rock, and I had soon found myself more at ease on mountain tracks than on the streets of
Milan. For ten months of the year I felt constrained in stiff,
good clothes, trapped within a system of authority and rules
that had to be obeyed; in the mountains I divested myself of
everything, and freed my true nature. It was a different kind
of freedom than that of someone who is free to travel and
meet people; or to spend a night drinking, singing, and court-
ing women; or to seek out companions with whom to em-
bark on some great adventure. These are all freedoms that I
appreciate so much so that at twenty it seemed important to

me to explore them for all they were worth. But at thirty I had almost forgotten what it was like to be alone in a forest, or to immerse myself in a river, or to run along the edge of a crest beyond which there is only sky. I had done these things, and they were my happiest memories. To me the young urban adult I had become seemed like the exact opposite of that wild boy, and hence the desire grew to go in search of him. It wasn't so much the need to leave as the desire to return; not to discover an unknown part of myself, but to recover an old and deep-seated one I felt that I had lost.

I had saved some money, enough to live on for a few months without working. I looked for a house that was far from any center of population, and as high up as possible. There are no vast wilderness spaces in the Alps—but I didn't need an Alaska for the experience I was longing for. I found the place I was seeking in the spring, in the valley adjacent to the one where I'd grown up: a cabin of wood and stone about six thousand feet above sea level, where the last conifer trees gave way to summer pastures. A place I'd never been to before, but one that I knew well, since it was just on the other side of the mountains I used to explore as a boy. It was about six miles from the nearest town, and a few minutes away from a village that would fill with people in summer and winter, but that was deserted when I reached it on the 25th of April. The fields were still dormant, tinged with the browns and ochres of the thaw; the slopes in the shadow of the mountains were still covered in snow. I left the car at the end of the asphalt road. I loaded my rucksack onto my shoulders and headed along the mule track, climbing through a wood and then a snow-covered pasture up to a cluster of huts, which were little more than ruins, except for the one that had been restored and that I'd rented. At the front door I turned around: there was nothing in the vicinity except the woods, the meadows, and those abandoned ruins; on the horizon the mountains that enclose the Valle d'Aosta in the south, toward Gran Paradiso; and then a fountain carved out of a tree trunk, the remains of a drystone wall, and a gurgling stream. This would be my world for an as yet unspecified amount of time, since I had no idea what it had in store for me. That day the sky was a funereal gray: a freezing cold morning, devoid of light. I had no intention of submitting myself to any kind of torture. If I found it to be good up there, then I'd stay—but it was also possible that I might plunge into even deeper despair, in which case I was ready to make my escape. I had brought books and notebooks with me. I hoped to start writing again, eventually. Right then I was cold, I had to put on a sweater and light the fire. So I pushed the door open and entered my new home.

SPRING

*Season of Solitude
and Observation*

Houses

There is something moving about opening a mountain cabin in the spring. I was throwing open doors to rooms that had been shut for months, with the ice their only master and the skylights blocked by snow. I passed a finger over the surface of a table, a chair, a shelf on which a layer of dust had settled, like forgotten ash from a chimney. Do houses have a way of sensing the passage of time? Or is a winter for them the same as an instant? I thought about the day, ten years previously, when I had left for the last time through that other door, looking lingeringly at everything. Now the sense of return was more olfactory than visual: it was the fragrance of the resin that reassured me that I was home again. I asked the house if the winter had been particularly hard. I imagined it moaning and creaking during January nights, when the temperature at that altitude drops below zero, then soaking up the pallid March sun, walls tepid now,

11

the snow dripping through the guttering. If the purpose of a house is to be lived in, I thought, then perhaps it experienced its own kind of happiness, knowing that once again someone was going back and forth carrying wood, lighting the stove, washing their hands in the kitchen. In this way the water that came from snow and rock was starting to flow through the walls again like sap in a tree. The fire was the lifeblood in a body.

In a story that I love called "My Four Houses," Mario Rigoni Stern revisits the stages of his life via the houses that he lived in. They were not all real houses: you can dwell in a house by imagining it, or by borrowing it from someone else's memory. The first house was a lost one: the ancestral home of the Sterns, four hundred years old and destroyed during the Great War. Born in 1921, Mario learned about it through the stories of his elders. It was the place he regretted not having been born in, to have this link between his family and the land, the patriotic feeling that for mountain folk does not belong to the nation but to a language, to the names of things and places, to seasonal tasks and to the proper way of doing them. The second was a real house, that of his childhood, full of secret corners like all the houses in which we were children. The third was a house of the mind: confined to a prison camp in 1945, Mario had found a piece of paper and a pencil and spent long, famished days designing a mountain cabin. He imagined it in a clearing where he would live by hunting, in solitude, with books for company, in order to cure himself of the war—like Nick Adams in Hemingway's "Big Two-Hearted River." For a long time that drawing kept him from despair. The fourth house was the one he actually built and lived in for fifty years with "my wife, my books, my pictures, my wine, and my memories," with its woods in front of his window, its beehives, its fields grazed by deer, its kitchen garden, and its woodpile.

I imagine that it must give you a great sense of peacefulness, living in a house built with your own hands. I did not have that privilege: the hut I was in had been built by mountain folk, who knows when, to house both animals and people during the pasture season, and done up ten years previously with modern conveniences. It was a house with only two rooms: below, where the stable used to be, there was a bathroom and a bedroom with a wardrobe, a chest, and a stove; above it was the kitchen, a sofa, a table with two benches and a chair. But the walls of uncut stone had not changed from when they were first built; touching them I wondered how many other hands had passed over them, how much woodsmoke, animal breath, steam rising from polenta and milk. Here and there, driven between one stone and the next, there were large nails, or half-charred wooden stakes. What was hung there, and who was it who'd hammered them in? It was a house infested with ghosts, but it was not frightening: it seemed a little as if I were living alongside those mountain folk, getting to know them through their spaces and the shapes of things there, the soot which still blackened that piece of wall.

The house in which I spent my summers as a child had been built as a hotel in 1855, but it was already a ruin during my childhood. It emerged outside the village, at the top of an avenue of beech trees, at the foot of a waterfall that became turbulent with end-of-summer rains. A plaque on the cracked plaster façade commemorated the sojourn of Queen Margaret of Savoy, when the mechanic's office was still the ballroom, and the roof, now invaded by weeds, was the terrace on which afternoon tea was served. The hotel had been open until the nineteen thirties but had been occupied by the Germans during the war and then sold, and fifty years later it had acquired the look of a gloriously dilapidated manor house. It belonged to two elderly sisters who had subdivided it into lodgings, earning them something from the summer rentals and remaining shut for the rest of the year. Devoid of maintenance or heating, every winter it suffered further decline. The snowfalls of April 1986 delivered the coup de grâce: an avalanche hit a section of the front of the building, and a whole wing was subsequently declared in danger of collapse. By the following summer large cracks had appeared in the remaining walls, and for years the nettles proliferated in the rubble that no one had been paid to remove. But what I remember more than the ruin is my astonishment at finding snow at the beginning of July—piled so high, so frozen and hard as to become a slide for toboggans. From then on, that summer would always be known as *the summer of the avalanche.*

Arriving from the city it seemed as if we were entering another era. An era in which kitchens had draining boards made of stone, and baths and basins of white enameled iron. On the ceiling, in the attic where I slept, the names of two girls were carved: Angela and Maddalena. Knowing that the servants used to lodge in those rooms, I wondered if at the beginning of the last century Angela and Maddalena had been maids in the service of some aristocratic lady or other—and I imagined their discussions in bed at night before falling asleep. I don't know if houses have souls, but I know that in that house I left a good part of mine: for twenty years from 1979 I lived there for two months of every year. With the end of the twentieth century came the end of the old hotel: sold, demolished, and replaced by a condominium. And so of that place, as Mario Rigoni Stern has it, "only my words now remain."

I thought of the summer of the avalanche as I looked at the patches of snow in the pasture in front of the cabin. Though protected by the shadow cast by the woods, each day they melted a little more: rivulets of water rushed down the field, exposing a black, humid soil, and grass that looked burned. Small birds with white bellies and dark backs lingered there, pecking at the ground on the margins of the snow. I had taken a book to help identify them, and I was almost certain they were alpine finches, "looking for the larvae of insects," as it was written there, "in the soil saturated by snow-melt, making their nests in the cavities of rocks or in the walls of huts." In fact, two had made a nest precisely in the gable end of mine, in that dark, protected corner between beam and roof. They flew back and forth between meadow and nest, keeping me company when I had lunch sitting at a table in front of the window.

In the afternoon a thick mist would arise: I could see it advance from the valley below, climbing up the meadows and woods until it enveloped everything. I remained immersed in that white blanket until it became dark. There was no moon or any stars at night, just rain mixed with a little snow that began to fall as I retired to bed.

At night I would struggle to get to sleep. Unused to the altitude, my heart beat more rapidly than normal and seemed to drum in my chest. Sounds are not like smells, it takes time to let oneself be lulled by them and not be startled by every new noise. So with eyes wide open I stared at the ceiling and thought: that's the noise made by embers being consumed, squeaking in the fireplace. That's the sound of the old fridge starting up. This is the rain on the stone roof. And these steps outside, at almost three in the morning, what are they? They were circling around the house, they were near the door, and in the city, one would have instinctively suspected it was a thief. Up there I had to resort to the most rational part of my being in order to convince myself that this visitor was only a wild animal in search of food. It made little difference: I could not close my eyes for the rest of the night, not until the first light of dawn prompted me to give in and get up to put the coffee on the stove.

Topography

Élisée Reclus, the nineteenth-century geographer and anarchist who suffered long years in exile on account of his ideas, writes that "from every peak, every ravine, every slope, the mountain landscape shows itself in a new relief, with a different aspect. The mountain is an entire range of mountains in itself; in the same way that in the sea every wave is made up of innumerable small irregular waves. To grasp the architecture of the mountain in its entirety you need to study it, walk it in every sense, clamber over every slope, penetrate into even the narrowest gorge. As with everything, it is infinite for anyone who wants to know it in its entirety."

This was the spirit in which I began my explorations. I took the path that began at the cabin and started following it to see where it led. I crossed a wood of larch, their tall, bare trunks alternating every so often with the green of a younger fir. A little farther up, the trees began to thin out; in the pastures exposed to the sun the first crocuses were already emerging, but I only needed to change sides, from south to west, and the grass was replaced by snow. Water was gushing everywhere, as if the entire mountain was saturated with it. From a hole between the exposed roots of a larch came murky torrents of mud. Where the path curved toward the north I sank to my waist in snow, and decided to turn back just as soon as I'd extracted myself. I descended in leaps and bounds, shouting like a yeti. I had not yet started talking to myself, but I liked to sing loudly; songs about love, about mountains, about struggles. I hadn't seen a living soul for a week, and this is how I kept myself company.

I had thought that the feeling of solitude would have grown with time, but the opposite occurred: after the first days of disorientation I was full of things to do. Studying the map of the region, cataloging animals and flowers, gathering wood from the forest, conducting experiments with the resin of firs, cutting the grass around the cabin. The melting snow gifted me many surprises: the skull of a marmot, the charcoal remains of an open-air fire, grooves left by tractor tires. The mousehole of a tiny mouse just emerged from hibernation gave me courage: if he had made it, I thought, after spending six months under the snow, then my season under the sun would be a breeze.

As for the map that I was unfolding, it started just on the other side of the front door and gradually extended as I discovered my surroundings. I proceeded by way of explorations, readings, archaeological findings, and uncertain deductions. The place in which I lived was a minuscule village called Fontane. I occupied the first in a row of four south-facing mountain huts, or cabins, at the top of a valley traversed by a stream without a name. Once, when these high mountain homesteads were still farms, a mule track used to reach up to a village that was inhabited all year round. It was dug into the earth and contained by drystone walls, so that the animals going along it could not invade the pastures. Now it was still visible at just a few points as a three-foot-wide trench skirting the wood, flanked every so often by piles of white stones shaped with mallet and chisel by ancient herders. The stream below, which had given rise to the village, had not merited a name on account of its brief length: I measured it in paces and counted no more than a hundred. It bubbled up from a spring in the middle of the pasture and threw itself into another stream a little farther down. It flowed over fine gravel, with blue and white reflections, remarkably similar to the bed of a river. Next to the stream, corresponding to each cabin, there was a small, stone construction. These were the cellars into which the milk was deposited after milking: the running water refrigerated it, allowing the cream that would be turned into butter to form. In my cellar I had an electric pump that took water from the stream and brought it into the house. Although I washed my hands and drank like any city dweller, that is to say by turning a tap and taking as much hot or cold water as I pleased, when doing so I always remembered that this water originated from there, from the white and blue gravel amid the grass, and in the taste of it at night it seemed like I could detect brine.

The land that surrounded me, rich in springs and well-positioned in the sun, had for many centuries been cleared of trees, freed from stones, and terraced where necessary—to cultivate rye and raise livestock at first, and then to create ski slopes. Up until the 1950s it was difficult to find a single tree in those parts, or to see a wild animal: I have seen old photographs in which the cultivated fields stretched up to unthinkable altitudes, and the whole mountain had the appearance of a well-kept lawn. After the war, however, the exodus from the highlands had started, and the woods had reconquered the land. The field near the cabin had been re-planted about fifty years earlier: the larches were still quite young, all the same size and spaced so that the grass could continue to grow at their feet. Finally, between the 1970s and 1980s, a section of those trees had been felled to make way for the pistes that cut the flanks of the mountains like the tracks left in the wake of avalanches. The pylons of chairlifts had begun to appear, certain irregular slopes had been flat-tened, and the place had taken on its current appearance.

Why did this history interest me so much? Because I needed to repeat to myself something very simple: the land-scape that surrounded me, with its authentically wild ap-pearance, with its trees, meadows, and streams, was in fact the product of human endeavor—it was a landscape as arti-ficial as that of a city. Without human habitation, nothing up there would have had the shape that it now possessed. Not even the stream, or certain majestic trees. Even the meadow in which I would lie down to sun myself would have been thickly forested, made impenetrable by fallen trunks and branches, by moss-covered monoliths and a dense under-growth of juniper, bilberry, and intricately entangled roots. There is no such thing as *wilderness* in the Alps, only a long history of human presence that is experiencing today an era of abandonment. Some suffer it like the death of a civiliza-tion; for my part I found myself actually rejoicing when finding a stone building swallowed by undergrowth, a tree that jutted where grain had once grown. But then it wasn't my history that was disappearing. I, who fantasized that wolves and bears might return, had no roots up there, and nothing to lose if the mountain finally liberated itself from mankind.

So my explorations took on the character of an investigation, an attempt to read the stories written on the terrain. In less poetic terms, I was collecting refuse. An old half-rotten wooden pail buried in a dunghill, a rusty lock. The history that interested me was entirely human: why, for instance, did the cabin behind mine have an extension to one side? Perhaps things had prospered at some point, and the farmer had needed a more spacious stable? It was the largest of them all, but also the most austere: tiny windows, three planks joined together to serve as a balcony. The third hut had its floor plan inverted and was turned to face north. Here too there must have been a reason for giving up the sun: a boundary dispute, perhaps? Then came the fourth cabin, which was the most well maintained and perhaps the most recent of the three. It had a small balcony with some attempt at decoration, glazed windows and even plastered external walls—a roughcast mixture with a few lumps here and there, of a dirty white that I really liked. Outside, there were two rickety enclosures for chickens, rabbits, or some other barnyard animal. Since the little village was distributed along a slight incline, the white building dominated the others from above: the one that was back to front, the one that had the large stable, and mine too, which as compensation had uninterrupted views.

Looking at them I would sometimes wonder if there had ever really been a period when Fontane was inhabited. I struggled to imagine it, because since I was a child all I'd ever seen in the mountains were ruins. I had the impression that the present, up there, had for a long time consisted of a mound of potsherds that was now impossible to put together again. All you could do was turn them over in the palm of your hand and speculate as to what they had been used for, which was what tended to happen if I moved a rock and found beneath it a wooden handle, a large bent nail, a tangle of metal twine, a rusted shovel.

Even though it seemed faintly comical, each of the four huts had its own postal number. At some stage a council bureaucrat must have been given the task of registering all the buildings, and so even the dilapidated huts scattered across the mountainside had a plaque with a number on it. Mine had the number 1. One of these days, I thought, I'll go down to the nearest town and send myself a postcard addressed to *Number 1, Fontane*, and then come back to wait for the postman to charge up the path. The cabin with the large stable had the number 2, the back-to-front one was 3, the white plastered one 4. But only the dormice and badgers that every so often I heard moving lived there. I was the entire population. Like Crusoe on his desert island, "I was lord of the whole manor; or, if I pleased, I might call myself king or emperor over the whole country which I had possession of." I represented, at the same time, the most eminent inhabitant and the most fallen on hard times, the aristocratic landowner and the faithful caretaker, the innkeeper and the drunk, the judge and the village idiot. I had as a result of this many versions of myself to contend with, so would sometimes go out for a walk through the woods in the evening, in order to be on my own for a while.

Snow

One morning in mid-May I woke up under snow. The violets were already flowering in the meadows, but by midday everything around me had turned white again. A storm like a summer one, with thunder and lightning, had brought the winter back to those parts. I stayed the whole day indoors with the stove lit, reading and gazing outside. I was gauging the layer of snow that was accumulating on the balcony: one, two . . . five inches. I wondered what would become of the flowers, insects, and birds that I had seen, feeling at this abrupt interruption of spring something like a sense of injustice on their behalf. I found the passage in which Rigoni Stern classifies late snowfalls: *snow of the swallow* in March, *cuckoo snow* in April, and what for him was the latest, *snow of the quail*. A cloud that descends from the north, a wind, a rapid drop in temperature, and suddenly there is snow in May. It only lasts a few hours, but it is enough to disturb nesting birds, to kill bees caught outside their hives, and to stress the female deer waiting to give birth.

Toward seven the sky cleared, and the white expanse became blinding as the sun emerged from behind the clouds shortly before sunset. I put on my jacket and climbing boots and went out to look around. In the snow I found the tracks of many wild animals: a hare, a pair of deer, countless birds, as well as other prints that I could not identify. I was struck to discover that all this activity had been going on while inside the house I had felt so mournfully alone. They had been there all the time, monitoring me, scenting me, keeping an eye on my movements, while I instead had eyes that saw nothing, gazing at the wood through my window without noticing anything. I wondered if in time I would learn how to get close to them—whether they would slowly come to trust me. For the moment all I could do was follow some tracks, choosing the hare's for preference: they were V-shaped prints that seemed to progress by leaps, starting from a juniper bush near the mule track. They went in one direction before heading, to my astonishment, toward the cabin. The hare had circled around the old larch tree, gone to drink at the basin, and had even jumped onto the table that I'd placed on the grass. There was a single set of paw prints on it—it had needed only one leap to get up and down again. I imagined the hare looking around, reading the signs of my presence in the smoke from the chimney, in the scythe and the saw hanging by the woodshed, in the blanket draped on the balcony. Eventually, it had gone over the wooden fence, receding toward the stream. No new snow had fallen on the prints, so rather than me pursuing her, the hare had come to seek me out.

During the snowfall I had heard a loud crash, like a nearby clap of thunder. Later, when I went to check in the woods, I found a fallen larch. The trunk had split at the height of a man, causing a long, irregular fracture that continued for three to six feet. It had a strange effect on me, seeing that tree lying on the ground, helpless but still alive. Its bud-covered branches were sinking into the snow, and I thought I could hear its death throes like those of an animal. It was precisely the new leaves that betrayed it, the ones that had grown in the last month: in the winter the larch is bare, retaining little of the snow that falls on its branches. Now, instead, the heavy wet flakes had accumulated in huge quantities in its dense canopy of needles. So a tree that had survived the long freeze had succumbed to the last, unforeseen, and fatal snowfall of May.

While I moved around it I saw a small bird in the snow. It was struggling to move, and I thought it must have fallen from its nest with the moribund tree. When I picked it up it tried beating its wings in my hand, then either calmed down or became paralyzed with fear, I couldn't say which. It was the first living thing I'd had any contact with in weeks, and it moved me; I did not realize that I was condemning myself to an inevitable loss. I could feel its accelerated heartbeat in the palm of my hand, the tickling of its claws on my skin. Everything will be all right, I told it. Don't worry, I'll look after you. In the house I laid a rag in the bottom of a shoe box and lowered the bird onto it. What could the diet of such a small one consist of? Given the snow that was outside, I could not even go looking for an insect or worm. So I tried to feed it breadcrumbs, discovering that it accepted them and managed to swallow a couple before falling asleep. But appetite and sleep were only illusions of vital signs. When I went back to check on the bird it was lying on its side: still breathing, but in a completely unnatural position. It did not open its eyes again. Before night fell it was dead, and I put it back close to the fallen larch, where during the night it would perhaps become a meal for a fox or for a crow. Leaving it for them to take seemed more fitting than burying it in a hole in the ground.

The next morning I was still thinking about the bird, drinking my coffee and watching the snow melting with the first sun, when I caught sight of a man coming up the path. I leaned out of the doorway to welcome him, but my excitement was such that I might just as well have run out to greet him. It's difficult to explain the effect a visit has when it comes after a period of complete solitude: for me it had only been two weeks, and yet my heart started to beat faster on seeing that man approach. It was Remigio, my landlord. He had come to see if the snow had caused me any problems, and if I had enough wood to keep warm. I had no idea what he made of my presence up there: during our only meeting I had told him that I wrote, and that I had come there to work. He had not seemed particularly impressed. Wasting few words, he had shaken my hand and given me the keys to the cabin as if it wasn't even his.

On this occasion he was more talkative. I invited him in for a coffee and we chatted for a while. When he saw the books that I'd brought with me I discovered that he was a reader too: we talked about Erri De Luca and Mauro Corona, then leafed through my guides to woodland animals and forest trees—and I ended up lending him the stories of Rigoni Stern that I was so attached to, because from the outset up there they had helped me to see and to hear. Remigio listened attentively, and when talking he chose his words carefully. He appeared to be in his forties, but his tanned skin and gray hair made for a strange contrast, giving an impression of a man who was at the same time both old and young. Getting to know him I would later discover that this was an accurate enough reflection of his character.

Later he returned with a chainsaw and together we cut up the fallen larch. There was only the odd patch of snow left from the previous day. We piled the thick logs up against the cabin wall that faced west; I would split them at my leisure and stack them to dry. If summer does its work I thought, watching him go, I will have good wood to burn in September, and perhaps a friend with whom to share the pleasures of the fireside.

Vegetable Garden

After getting in the wood supply there was another task that I wanted to complete. I had been mulling over this idea for a while now, and the meeting with Remigio had given me a decisive push. One morning at the end of May, while waiting for his arrival with the tools, I went ahead and built a bench by hand: I took two large stones from the mule track and laid between them a plank that I'd found in the woods, gray now due to all the sun and rain that it had taken, the veins of the wood standing out like those of old men. Then I sat down to read the chapter in *Walden* on the field of beans:

> What was the meaning of this so steady and self-respecting, this small Herculean labour, I knew not. I came to love rows of beans, though so many more than I wanted. They attached me to the earth, and so I got

strength like Antaeus. But why should I raise them? Only heaven knows. This was my curious labour all summer— to make this portion of the earth's surface, which had yielded only cinquefoil, blackberries, johnswort, and the like, before, sweet wild fruits and pleasant flowers, produce instead this pulse. What shall I learn of beans or beans of me? I cherish them, I hoe them, early and late I have an eye to them; and this is my day's work.

Charmed by Thoreau's words, I scrutinized the meadow that went down to the stream. I lit on a small patch just below the fountain: it was rich soil, fertilized annually by shepherds. It absorbed sunlight from nine in the morning until eight at night, and the water needed to irrigate it was right there, just a few steps away. Already I could almost see the red of tomatoes and the yellow of zucchini flowers. I was impatient to begin my life as a farmer.

Remigio soon enough extinguished the colors of my fantasy. Up there I could forget about tomatoes and such, he explained, it was already quite an achievement to get leafy vegetables to grow: lettuce, cabbage, the tops of beets, spinach, celery. With luck I might be able to cultivate some stunted carrots, radishes, broccoli, leeks. Was this still all right? I replied that, as far as I was concerned, it was fine. Then I started a Rotavator for the first time in my life—

a little motorized plow, about the size of a lawn mower, the blade of which digs into the ground about a foot deep, turns over clods of earth, and roughly crumbles them into pieces. In this way we plowed a rectangle thirteen feet by twenty.

It was only the beginning of my labors. Having broken the crust, for the rest of the day I hoed the ground and raked the soil beneath. I removed stones and pulled up roots, discovering that those graceful flowers had powerful bulbs, hidden at great depths to survive the freeze, and were impossible to eradicate. I crumbled the more compressed clods with my hands, then went down to the village to buy some plants. To protect them from the deer I even built a fence with four larch panels. I tied a strong net around them and was satisfied at how my little vegetable plot was developing—but when I sat down at last to admire it the voice of Thoreau evaporated, and in its place the notes of Fabrizio De André's "Il suonatore Jones" echoed. The song, that is, in which he says that liberty sleeps in cultivated fields. Suddenly the six mounds of turned earth seemed like so many grave mounds. It was my freedom that was buried there. I felt a little depressed, so I put away my hoe and rake, picked up the walking stick, and decided to go for a walk.

I went higher than I had pushed myself as yet, and at a

certain point abandoned the path, since the whole mountainside that was in shadow was still snowbound. There was no one around: the low-hanging clouds, the threat of rain, and the cold had kept hikers away. I plunged down into a fir copse, with the intention of crossing it and climbing back up the valley to the sunlit side, where the slopes were already free of snow. At the end of the wood I found a small wooden bridge, a village consisting of ten or so houses on the banks of the stream. Almost all of them had ruined roofs, the wall facing the mountain distended in that swollen-belly shape that presages collapse. Overcoming the atmosphere of abandonment, I entered one of the buildings that was still standing. In its only room I found a small wooden bed, a bench, a wonky stool. On the floor there were more recent signs: meat and sardine tins, large wine bottles, a shirt reduced to rags, the rubbish of some shepherd who had camped there without caring. There was an oppressive smell of mold, and I returned to the open air with relief.

Going up the slope I reached the summit of a peak, and finally on the other side I saw the lake that I'd heard about. It was covered in a layer of ice and surrounded by snow: only the odd rock protruded every so often on the steeper banks. I had thought of reaching it, but seeing it from above like this, frozen in that overshadowed basin, made me change my mind. So I lay down on the ground and remained up there, my hands beneath my head, to contemplate the rain-swollen clouds. Glimpses of blue sky appeared between them. Two eagles wheeled around a summit, perhaps hunting the newborn young of chamois and alpine ibex. The crows, less noble and more piteous, flew over the deserted *alpeggi*—the high alpine pastures and summer farmsteads—searching for remains of food, or for some carcass of a rodent that had failed to survive the winter.

Then the two eagles came closer, at lower altitude, and I realized that they were not a pair but an adult and eaglet. What I was watching seemed to be a flying lesson. The adult repeated a very elaborate maneuver: it remained stationary in midair, supported on a thermal, then suddenly folding its wings and performing a body twist, horizontally, it precipitated uncontrollably. It looked like the signature move of a stunt pilot. About a foot lower down it extended its wings and braked the fall, catching the current again and returning to its original altitude. The young eagle watched attentively, and I thought that soon it would be his turn. I wondered whether the adult was the mother or the father.

On the way back it began to rain again, and it reduced the snow to slush. It was the perfect day for an outing, clearly.

But with damp hair, sodden feet, and the windchill that froze them, I told myself that at least I was recovering my good humor. I came across a clearing populated by marmots, where I was welcomed by a thicket of whistles and a general stampede. There was one that seemed braver than the rest: while its companions ran for cover inside the first available hole, it lingered at the entrance of its burrow and looked back at me. Very slowly, trying not to make any sudden movements, I went toward it. When I was ten feet away it vanished into the hole, so I stopped, lay down my stick, and sat down cautiously. I thought I would sing it a song, and since it had been playing in my head all morning I chose De André: *In a whirl of dust the others saw drought, and I saw Jenny's skirt as she danced, thirty years ago.*

All it took was two verses for the marmot's snout to pop out from the burrow: it was listening to me, scenting me, trying to understand what kind of enemy I could be. I carried on singing: *I felt my land vibrating with sounds, it was my heart—so why cultivate it again, why think it could be better?*

Every so often the marmot would pop back in, but for the most part it just stayed there watching me. Who is this? And what's he up to? *Freedom, I've seen it sleep in cultivated fields, with sky and money, with sky and love, protected by a barbed wire fence. Freedom, I've seen it wake every time I've played, for a swish of girls at a dance, for a drunken friend.*

I sang it three times in a row, and the marmot kept listening. Then I got up and it immediately hid. I picked up my stick and started to walk back down toward my little vegetable patch.

Night

I continued to sleep badly. Despite the fact that more than a month had passed, I still found myself waking in the middle of the night, eyes blinded but ears attuned to every creaking board, every rustle that came from outside. I have never had a good relationship with the dark. As a child I was terrified of it, spending nights prey to a sense of impending disaster. In the city the streetlights kept me company: my window faced an avenue on which the flow of traffic hardly ever ceased, and due to a mirror effect I would see on the ceiling the headlights of cars scurrying, the yellow of the streetlights flashing, the blue of ambulances, the green light of an all-night pharmacy. Every so often an alarm or a siren would sound, the high-pitched calls of birds above the continuous murmuring of the river. It calmed me to feel the life flowing around me, its noises lulling me to sleep.

In the cabin I plunged back into childhood fears: when the moon waned, the darkness was absolute, and the silence so deep as to hurt my ears, strained as they were to catch every sound. I managed to hear the water flowing in the fountain. The wind that moved the tops of the larch trees. The calling of a deer in the forest, which is not at all as one might imagine it to be. It is nothing like a bellowing—it resembles instead a fit of hoarse coughing, the barking of a dog that has lost its voice. They were the wild animals and I was the predator, but in my bed the darkness reversed these roles. At five the first light came as a relief: the birds were starting to sing, life was beginning to course again in the world, and my vigil was no longer required. Then, like a night watchman who has completed his rounds, I was overwhelmed by a leaden sleep from which I would wake befuddled midmorning.

So it was that one evening I put on two sweaters, filled a flask with wine, grabbed my sleeping bag, and decided to camp outside. It was a kind of shock therapy. At around nine I lit a fire against a section of mule-track wall, whittled some willow sticks until they were sharply pointed, and used them as skewers for grilling pieces of sausage. For bread I had a crisped flatbread, one of those I'd cooked after kneading flour and water. Out there in front of the fire a gourmet meal was served: when the meat was ready

I slipped it off the skewer with the bread and accompanied each mouthful with a sip of wine. At ten, darkness having fallen, I unrolled the sleeping bag and climbed inside. I discovered that I wasn't sleepy at all. So I sat up without leaving the sleeping bag, feeding the fire with the kindling I'd gathered in the woods. I stayed there to finish the wine, watching the wood burn.

On that strange night another experience came back to me, from many summers ago, that had begun in a village bar with my father and uncle. After dinner my father had talked about a mountain belonging to that region which used to be climbed in the dark in order to watch the dawn from its summit. It was approximately sixty-five hundred feet above the village, a four- to five-hour trek at a good pace. So, said my uncle, when do we leave? Let's do it. They'd had several rounds of grappa; I was fourteen and keen to prove my courage. I went with them. At midnight we took the path and spent the first hour of trekking stumbling over roots and stones, laughing and cursing, taking turns to light each other's way with the single torch we had between us. Then the wood came to an end, and with it the effect of the grappa. The two brothers no longer spoke, now all they did was puff and pant instead. Their throats must have been parched, and their legs made rubbery by the drink—but no one wanted to be the first to suggest that we should turn back. At no more than halfway, at about three o'clock, in the middle of the pastures, it seemed to us that we could hear the sound of an organ. Then we made out the glow coming from a small window. Who was playing the organ at three o'clock in the morning, in an isolated cabin at seven thousand feet? We were tired and freezing. So as not to frighten the musician, my father and uncle decided not to knock at his door, but to make their appearance singing at the top of their voices. Even in those conditions they retained their mischievous spirit. Before the front door of the cabin they began to sing an alpine chorus; after two stanzas the music stopped, a ground-floor light came on, and the owner of the house opened the door. He was a man in his sixties. He did not seem at all pleased to see us. It was obvious that he did not welcome company, but he forced himself to be hospitable: he made us hot tea, lent us another two torches, resisted our attempts at conversation, wished us a good journey, and saw us to the door. When we were farther along the path we heard him start playing again. Finally we really did reach the summit, but I do not remember anything about the dawn. Who was the mysterious musician? How on earth had he managed to transport an organ up there? Perhaps he too did not have a very good relationship with the dark. At the time he seemed eccentric to me, if not a complete madman of the mountains; now, instead, in front of that campfire I too would like to have been able to play like him. A guitar, or at the very least a harmonica. Singing by yourself really wasn't the same thing.

I opened my eyes again after a sleep of I didn't know how long. Half an hour, two, maybe even three . . . ? In the sky the moon had risen, and of my fire there remained only a pile of glowing embers. I caught the smell of ash and humid earth, felt the bitter aftertaste of wine, and beneath my back the sleeping bag sodden with dew. So I got up and went to wash my face at the fountain, the freezing water of the night having the instant effect of startling me awake. I was unsure whether to go to bed or rekindle the fire and wait there for the dawn that could not have been far off now. Still that old urge to prove one's virility; but if the enemy to be vanquished was my own self, then retreating from the fray and throwing myself under the covers might also constitute an authentic victory.

I had sat down on the steps of the cabin to decide what to do when I caught sight of a movement in the meadow. I turned toward the place where I'd been sleeping and saw the unmistakable profile of a fox. The sharp snout, the pricked ears, the bushiest of tails as long as its body. It had not noticed me: it was sniffing the ground around the campfire, searching for remnants of my supper, and I stood completely still, hoping to remain undiscovered for a little while longer. The moon above the meadow cast a gold light on everything. The fox scratched the earth near the embers and licked something, a small morsel of meat that had escaped me, or perhaps only some grease. Then suddenly, with no forewarning, perhaps because of a gust of wind carrying my scent, it raised its head and saw me. Its eyes reflected the glow of the embers. I must have been only a dark mass in the shadow cast by the house, and the fox took a few seconds to recognize me. That exchange of looks seemed to last an inordinate length of time. The fox was not frightened by it: perhaps over many nights she had become familiar with my smell. She lingered before unhurriedly trotting into the darkness. I went to collect the sleeping bag, hung it on the fence to dry, and then abandoned myself to my human bed.

Thoreau writes:

> I find it wholesome to be alone the greater part of the time. To be in company, even with the best, is soon wearisome and dissipating. I love to be alone. I never found the companion that was so companionable as solitude. We are for the most part more lonely when we go abroad

among men than when we stay in our chambers. A man thinking or working is always alone, let him be where he will. Solitude is not measured by the miles of space that intervene between a man and his fellows [...]

Society is commonly too cheap. We meet at very short intervals, not having had time to acquire any new value for each other. We meet at meals three times a day, and give each other a new taste of that old musty cheese that we are. We have had to agree on a certain set of rules, called etiquette and politeness, to make this frequent meeting tolerable and that we might not come to open war. We meet at the post, and at the sociable, and about the fireside every night; we live thick and are in each other's way, and stumble over one another, and I think that we thus lose some respect for one another [...]

I have heard of a man lost in the woods and dying of famine and exhaustion at the foot of a tree, whose loneliness was relieved by the grotesque visions with which, owing to bodily weakness, his diseased imagination surrounded him, and which he believed to be real. So also, owing to bodily and mental strength, we may be continually cheered by a like but more normal natural society, and come to know that we are never alone.

Neighbors

In June the shepherds came and my solitude changed.
They arrived in lorries, large trucks for transporting livestock that appeared one day at the end of the road. Ner-
vous from the journey, and excited perhaps to see all those
flowering meadows, the cows came rushing down the
ramps, poking each other with their horns, paying no attention to the boundaries of the fields and ending up hiding among the fir trees. The shepherds left them to their
own devices. Despite this motorized seasonal migration,
the oldest among the shepherds still wore velvet waist-
coats and felt hats, a costume that the younger ones had
replaced with waterproof overalls. All of them were looking at the mountains on the horizon as if they needed to
refamiliarize themselves with the landscape. They'd un-
dergone a relocation in the full sense of the term: they
changed houses for four months, transferring their animals

and families up there, going to a much harder life than the one they had in wintertime, and yet there was a gaiety in their gestures. They exchanged news with each other in dialect, laughing frequently. It seemed to me that the happiness of the animals had become infectious, and that it had been transmitted to the men as well: that climbing to the higher pastures was a homecoming for them too, perhaps to the places of their childhood or to the origins of their working lives.

So now I had something to observe apart from the clouds, which during those days were carriers of interminable rain. Not far from the cabin, on the other side of the valley in which I lived, was the alpeggio that I had thought was abandoned until the arrival of its owners: on that side, at the beginning of June, the yellow dandelions reigned, and if I woke early I could spy the old shepherd who was shifting the boundary of the pasture, moving the fence about three feet forward each day, in order to ration the grass. A little later the younger shepherd would open the door of the stable, and then seven calves and about thirty adult cows would rush down toward the new strip of tall grass. They were nearly all of a Red Pied Valdaostan breed, dominated by a few more agile and muscular black cows. By evening nothing remained of that grass. While I prepared my supper, an imperious lowing arose from the stable: three or four metal churns would appear in front of the entrance, and a 4×4 would arrive soon after to take them to the dairy. Only then was the working day at an end.

But the biggest change in my daily life was due to the dogs. Because I put aside crusts of cheese for them, they would come to find me several times a day—and to tell the truth, though it was hardly in keeping with mountain ways, I would sometimes give them the odd biscuit instead of the crusts, of the kind I took to calling *friends' biscuits*. Each dog had a bell hanging around its neck, thanks to which I could hear them coming from a long way off. Due to some kind of hierarchical arrangement between them, one of the three would always stay behind in the pasture, while the other two were free to roam until it was time to lead the cattle back to the stable. Then, called back by the young shepherd, they worked as a team: they circled the herd, barking, nipping the flanks of the lazier cows, and pursuing any that strayed, pushing them back toward the homestead. It was a wonderful sight to see them in action.

From the shouts of the cowherds I discovered that they were called Black, Billy, and Lampo (lightning). Black was the eldest, a great black mastiff with six toes on his back paws and his right ear torn off in one of his many fights. That's why I decided to call him Mozzo (a maimed one) instead of Black. You could tell that he was nearing the end of his working life: he preferred the shade of the fir trees to herding cows, and the scent of game that he followed lazily in the undergrowth. Billy was a German shepherd and a tireless worker, which is why the two of us crossed paths less frequently. When he came to see me he had a guilty look about him: he would take the salami rind and bolt immediately, rarely allowing himself to be stroked. Lampo was the youngest, a border collie with a passion for chasing larch sticks thrown far for him. He loved being scratched behind his ears and left on my hands a pleasant smell redolent of the stable. He was learning his trade, but he was still a novice and every so often would get into trouble.

One morning, in the middle of a torrential downpour, the seven calves mutinied and all went beyond the boundary of the field, throwing themselves on the tall grass as if it was a table set for a feast. At this point the young shepherd gave a loud whistle. Billy immediately darted out in pursuit, Lampo saw him go and ran after him, while Mozzo stayed behind watching from my balcony, alert but detached as was the custom of this old leader. I sat next to him to enjoy watching the maneuver. In the pasture Billy was bringing back the fugitives in a group, but then Lampo got too rough with one of the calves, biting and barking at him unnecessarily so that he made his escape again, followed by the six others. Billy rushed to retrieve them and the scene repeated itself. One of the dogs would catch them again only for the other to scare them away, and the bewildered calves kicked and ran in every direction.

By this stage Billy was soaked with rain; he looked at the calves, looked at his master, who was cursing and shaking his umbrella, then withdrew his labor and headed off toward the woods. The young shepherd was shouting his name, but Billy disappeared among the larch trees and was not seen again. Lampo was wagging his tail nearby, for him it was all a great game. The calves were having a slap-up feast in what should have been the next day's supply of grass. The rain was coming down with such force, threatening to sweep us all away, clearing us from the mountain like dry leaves, and on the balcony Mozzo finished his biscuit, stretched his back a little, and, grumbling, resigned himself to the idea that it was his turn now.

The next morning it was still raining, and I'd decided to prepare green tagliatelle. I gathered nettle leaves and wild spinach from around the cabin, let them sweat in the pan, and then chopped them before mixing in the eggs and flour. I had begun to stretch the pasta with the rolling pin when I heard a racket of bells and the shouts of a shepherd. I looked out of the window and caught sight of two calves careering downhill. The shepherd was not one of my neighbors, but the solitary and slightly lame one who would occasionally pass by on his tractor; he was the only one who deigned to greet me, even though we had never exchanged a single word. Hampered by his leg, he had not been able to run after the fugitives. I could see him up above, in the middle of the meadow, cursing and gesticulating wildly. I took off my apron, turned off the gas under the pan of water for the pasta, then picked up my stick and went outside dusted with flour as I was. I found the calves a little lower down, in a clearing in the middle of the wood. They were grazing calmly. I did not know whether they would obey me or not, I had only watched how it was done. I moved around the first one and tapped on its flank with the stick, and very slowly, reluctantly, he began to climb back up. The other one was following behind. Proud of my success, I guided them to Fontane and shut them into a corner between the fence and the cabin, then waited for the lame shepherd, hoping that he would get there soon. He appeared after a few minutes riding pillion on a motocross bike ridden by a friend of his. He secured the calves with a hemp rope and asked me how I had managed to catch them; I replied that it had been easy, that they'd done all the work themselves. He laughed at this, and I noticed that his canine teeth were missing. He said that on reflection he might be persuaded to take me on as a watchman.

His name was Gabriele. He was somewhere between forty and fifty years old; it was difficult to tell from his enormous hands, docker's physique, ragged clothes, unkempt beard, and sunburned skin. Seen up close, his limp was more conspicuous: he told me that the previous year the tractor's handbrake had failed and he had ended up under it while chopping wood, and now his left leg was held together by a metal plate and a few screws. He already knew all about me. At what time I lit the stove, how often I would go out into the vegetable patch to pull up weeds, and that I would go out walking almost every day. He would see me from above while leading the cows to pasture: his cabin was only a little farther up than mine, about fifteen minutes away by the path, and thanks to that morning's exploit I earned myself an invitation to supper that evening.

I wasn't cut out to be a hermit: I'd gone up there to be alone, yet I did nothing but seek company. Or perhaps it was the situation itself that made every encounter so desirable and precious. After almost two months in the cabin, my season of solitude was coming to an end with the spring.

At seven Mozzo came by searching for biscuits, looking me up and down while I put on my jeans and my best checked shirt. Used to seeing me in shorts and a sweater full of holes, he could not understand what was going on. What are you looking at? I asked. Can't I be invited to dinner once in a while? Then I laced my boots, picked up the bottle of Nebbiolo that I had kept for a special occasion, and headed for the path in the direction of my appointment.

SUMMER

*Season of Friendship
and Adventure*

Shepherd,
Where Are You Going?

So you're a subversive, he said, uncorking the wine, when I tried to explain what I had gone up there for. I had told him that I didn't like rules or bosses, and that in the city I felt caged; if to live in my own way I needed to be alone on a mountain, so be it, I accepted the solitude in exchange for the freedom it gave me. Gabriele completely understood the sentiment. It was only when I turned it into a political issue that he grimaced. He wore army surplus jackets, loathed foreigners (despite having only seen a couple in his entire lifetime), and liked to act tough when talking about women. And yet I was convinced that he was much more anarchistic than I was: he had neither a family nor a fixed job; no television, or car, or debt to a bank; no need of money except to buy food and drink; did not vote and could not be traced on the internet. He had never been included in any kind of poll or market survey, and he was representative of nothing.

A man such as he was, who had built a life on the margins and lived it his own way—he was by far the most subversive individual I could imagine in our current age, but I could hardly find a way of telling him so. Whenever I strayed into complicated areas of discussion he would scowl, and if I resorted to difficult words he would just stop listening. And so I gave in to him. Perhaps you're right, I said. I guess I really must be a subversive.

He did not say *le mucche* (the cows), he said *le baracche* (the old wrecks). Or if he was angry with them, *le baldracche* (the loose women). Not even these belonged to him: they sent them up to him from the plains to pasture in the mountains for the summer. In this way Gabriele turned a profit from the only things he had: a cabin, a tractor, a stable, some meadowland that was covered in snow for six months of the year. In wintertime he lived in a small room in the village and adjusted to being an employee, working on the ski slopes. But he disliked being down in the valley: he was too feral for urban life. He spoke only by shouting, as if there was always some actual distance between himself and everyone else. He could do nothing quietly. Just one of his fingers was as thick as two of mine, and everything became fragile in his hands. Sometimes he would be hired in the village, by the day, to demolish a wall or split a few cords of wood, but before nightfall he would return with his tractor to his cabin at seven thousand feet. Only up there did he find the space that he needed: he seemed to belong to the mountain in the same way that a random boulder or century-old larch did, raised in the middle of a pasture, exposed to the sun and wind.

Let's put the baracche to bed, he would say as evening approached. Then he would open the stable door wide and make a gap in the electric fence before patiently calling out to them. Come hi, come hi, come hi. One by one the animals would lethargically respond. For the next half hour, insults and loud slaps could be heard issuing from the stable: as soon as they were tethered the cows would begin to revolt, get into skewed positions and change places with each other, making it necessary to shove them into position with shoulder barges and drag them by their collars, in oppressive heat made humid by their breath and sweat. Then, luckily, Gabriele had a couple to milk and so calmed down again. It was a ritual that really helped him to relax. There are those who milk with their thumbs folded into the fist, he explained to me, using the knuckle to squeeze the udder—but he did not like this method because it was too crude. He preferred to use the palm of his hand. He would then leave the milk pail for the calves and the dog, keeping only a drop for himself, for his morning coffee. At that point we would finally shut the stable door and go to supper.

His home consisted of a wood-paneled room, ten feet by ten, a camp bed, a stove, no running water, and no bathroom. Around it there were six or seven dilapidated stone huts, one of which he used as a cellar, another as a woodshed. Inside, the room was bedecked with objects: on the walls a collection of cowbells and collars, cups won at the cattle show (or "battle of the cows"), naked pinups from the calendar of a tractor dealership. A small glass cabinet, a small piece of sixties furniture made of chipboard (sawed in half because it didn't fit), a much older cupboard, also small, consisting of just two shutters and a latch to enclose a niche in the rock. Wooden plates, a copper cauldron. Hanging above the stove were the tools for making cheese.

At supper he would frequently talk about past times. He was a naturally lively person, but abandonment made him melancholy: he remembered when he used to go up there with his mother and sisters, and now he was alone. Among the photos hung on the wall there was one of him with his wife and children—but fearing that this would be a painful trigger I preferred not to touch it. I asked instead about the photo of the black cow in which he was smiling with his arms around its neck. That was Morgana, his favorite, dispatched to the slaughterhouse many years ago now. The only thing she lacked, he told me, was the ability to speak. Now he had Lupo to keep him company, a sheepdog that followed him everywhere: sharp, reserved, affectionate, the most intelligent he'd ever had. Hearing himself mentioned by name, Lupo's ears pricked up from his bed near the stove, and looking up at us he came over for a pat and the crusts of the toma cheese.

In Gabriele's stories a lost world lived on—one in which, there in the village, each of the houses was inhabited and a hub of work. Men at work in the fields and in the stables, young boys in the pasture, women busying themselves with the farmyard animals. It was two hours by mule track to get to the village, and there was polenta and milk for both lunch and dinner. Hence his hatred for polenta, which he could not bear to eat anymore. Only a few days were required to forget civilization, to shed shoes and clothes and return to a more feral state. And yet he insisted on explaining that the shepherd, the *berger*, is the one with the sheep, and that there is a different word for the one who has cows: *vacher*, or cowherd. It's a not insignificant difference. The shepherd is nomadic, grazing and sleeping where chance takes him— the cowherd, on the other hand, is sedentary, with his own fields, a house, and a stable.

Then I discovered while chatting that he had never really witnessed that vanished world. The village was already deserted when he was a child. He played his games in its abandoned houses, with the help of the odd companion from some neighboring alpeggio. The populated mountain was not a memory of his, but a legend of a golden age with which to inspire dreams of happiness: he would like to have come up with his two sons of nineteen and twenty years old who worked as bricklayers, and to bring chickens, a donkey, a couple of goats, and a pig to butcher in the autumn. He often talked of buying some animals, so as to have the wherewithal to be self-sufficient. All he had, instead, was grass with which he fattened other people's cows, and endless nights of wide-eyed dreams.

Since I liked cooking and he didn't, and neither of us really minded having company at dinner, we would sometimes arrange things in the following way: I would climb up to his house at around seven, retrieve the big key from its place under a rock, and go inside to light the stove. Then I would go to wash the dishes in the fountain where Gabriele had placed a bath to use as a basin for himself, his clothes, and for the pots and pans. There I would find soap, a brush, a metal scourer. It had a strange effect on me to be scrubbing the pans in the light of the sunset, and using freezing cold water and no soap meant that there was a lot of scrubbing to do. But where could I have found a better washing place? The marmots scrutinized me while I filled a pan with water for the pasta. From the wood the muzzle of a deer emerged. When I went back into the house the stove was well lit and I would turn on the radio, put the water on to boil, and sit down to peel the potatoes. Spaghetti with a tomato sauce, boiled potatoes and cheese, and the occasional piece of sausage made up our daily diet. On his way back from the stable Gabriele would pass by the cellar where he stored four demijohns of Barbera—enough for the whole summer if one of them hadn't been smashed in an attempt to uncork it with a punch. The same thing happened to the windshield of the tractor, turning it into a coupe. These, for him, were typical misadventures.

When it was his turn to come down to me, he would always sit in the same place, on the bench with his shoulders against the wall so as to have a good look at the house. You really know how to live well, he would say, as he looked around—because I had a real kitchen, a fridge, and even a sofa, a bathroom, running water, walls that were upright, and a roof that was intact, so that I did not have to take shelter under the table when it rained. He always brought me a piece of cheese and a large bottle of wine. Once he arrived with a roast chicken picked up who knows where. Another time, when he'd been working for a friend down in the valley, he came back with eleven pounds of rice and a repertoire of brand-new anecdotes: the evening spent at the nightclub with the Russian girls, the line of John Deere tractors that he had seen at the farm, the boy who had made him laugh by asking why they called him Rambo, and was it because he was so strong.

At the end of the evening he had an elaborate way of leaving. It was a kind of ceremony, and it took me some time to figure out how it worked. The first time he said: Good, I think I'll go now; so I would get up to open the door and say goodbye. He gave me an odd look and asked: Are you in a hurry?

Me?—No, I said. I shut the door and sat back down again.

That night I discovered that before actually leaving he had to say *I'll be off now* at least five or six times, and in the meantime an hour might pass, with another story, another bottle of wine. And naturally I learned to do the same. When I was up at his place, at a certain point in the evening I would stretch a little, glance toward the darkness outside, and say: *I'll be off now.*

Have another piece of cheese, Gabriele would reply, completely ignoring what I'd said. Shall we drain another bottle?

Why not, I would say (up there, food and drink regress to

an elemental state: you *murder* pork ribs, you *drain* a bottle of wine), and I would delay my departure by a few more glasses.

On the 29th of June, St. Peter's day, the patron saint of alpeggi, we climbed up to the stable together after supper. Gabriele had spent the afternoon loading the trailer with dried branches that were now stacked up next to a huge boulder. There was a heap over three feet high. Toward ten o'clock he lit the fire in the style of mountain folk: he poured half a jerrican of gas over it and struck a match. The fire blazed instantly. With the deep silence around us I realized for the first time how deafening a fire can become, how unbearably hot within a radius of about ten feet. We sat on the grass to watch the dark outlines of the mountains, looking out for other fires like our own. We counted three, four, five, some of them in places that we could not even name. Those trembling yellow pilot lights seemed to say *I am here. And so am I, so am I, so am I.* A constellation made up of solitudes that barely shone for a few moments, then became fainter and were extinguished, one after another. Our fire too was silenced. I began to feel the breeze in the grass again, the gurgling of the stream, the sighs of the cows ruminating in the stable.

Now that I had become accustomed to the warmth of the fire I also realized that it was getting cold. As we were saying goodbye Gabriele loaned me a sweater and said: Go ahead, cut through the meadows. It was a great honor that he was granting me. Following the path would have resulted in a roundabout route, whereas by the meadows I would go straight down to Fontane. I descended in the dark, stretching my arms wide in the wind and feeling the grass spikes tickling the palms of my hands. Hurling their raucous calls the roe deer chased each other in the wood.

Hay

The month of July came. When the grass had become waist high and started to yellow, all over the meadows, mowers, tractors, trailers, hay-balers began to appear. Everyone worked at hay-baling, from the old to the youngsters of the alpeggi: a collective mobilization in the presence of which it was impossible to stand idly by, so I began to help Remigio and his mother. It wasn't that I was missing the family left behind in the plains. She was almost eighty, thin as a rake, tireless, gnarled like the bark of a tree; I was a well-meaning city-dweller with delicate skin: we made an odd couple behind the tractor that her son was driving. We baled the hay in the late afternoon, when the hay mown the day before had been dried by the sun. These days it was worth less than the effort it cost, but I could see how precious it was from her actions: she

69

went behind the tractor with a rake and did not leave behind a single blade of grass, while scolding me for all those I was losing. From behind the wheel Remigio grinned. He didn't much mind that someone else should be subjected to this treatment instead of him. To begin with, his mother pointed out where I was going wrong, but then concluded that I just didn't know how to rake and assigned heavier work to me instead—loading the hay bales onto the trailer. This was work that suited me better: by the twine that cut into my hands I would lift two at a time and fling them on board before quickly jumping up after them to stack them properly. In this way I earned a little respect, sweating and covering myself in dust, acquiring a laborer's calluses and a farmer's sunburned neck, my skin irritated by the hay that scratched it.

Between one load and the next I would raise my head and look at the surrounding fields. The reddish brown of those not yet mowed, the gold where the hay was drying in the sun, the soft green that eventually replaced it. It was lovely to see the mountain tended like a garden, with the crocuses poking back up through the new grass, believing that spring had returned. Except that the crocuses of the thaw were white like the clouds of April, whereas these were violet and lilac like the skies of July, and now there were no larvae left—just the buzzing of insects in the full heat of summer. Every so often Remigio's mother would go to fetch some refreshments from the bar: an orange soda or some other fizzy drink, an ice-cream for herself.

Can't we have a beer? Remigio complained. Sitting on a bale of hay, surrounded by the chittering of grasshoppers, he regarded the can as if he hardly knew which side of it to open.

I hope you don't plan to get drunk, his mother would tersely reply. I was formally included in this sentiment, as perhaps were all men in general.

―――――

There was a hill in front of the place where we were working, a wide and gently sloping passage along which one walked to the neighboring valley, which I would occasionally glance at, thinking meanwhile of a certain person. He must still be living there, and still working as an alpine guide since I could not imagine him doing any other kind of job. His name was Lorenzo, Renzo for short, named after the patron saint of August and of many villages, and he was my mountaineering guru—the first to have tied me to his rope, to have shown me where to place my hands on the rock face, with a pair of crampons clasped to my feet so that I could follow him onto the glacier. But more than a school focused on equipment and techniques, alpinism had been for me as a child a way of confronting fear, exhaustion, and cold: it was about being far from home. It was also about physical pain, since as soon as I went above ninety-eight hundred feet I began to get altitude sickness: nausea churned my stomach, my eyes would glaze over, and I would be overwhelmed by great nostalgia, by something like a sense of being abandoned, that for me was the real mountain sickness. Renzo shared those moments with me. While I sobbed and vomited, he was the person who would speak kindly to me and convince me to go on. He was so good at this that I would have followed him anywhere.

Then our relationship had moved into a golden period. At sixteen I had got over my sickness and had begun to enjoy our adventures: every summer Renzo would lead a group of boys to a high-altitude refuge for a week of mountaineering training. We would clamber up using an ice ax and crampons on the seracs of Monte Rosa, lower ourselves down into the depths of the crevasses to simulate rescue operations, and run down the glacier dragging an imaginary casualty on a sled, being passed meanwhile by the serious collectors of peaks. We weren't interested in summits. Rock faces and crests were much more diverting—to climb them as if it were a game. I was strong now, I felt at home on the glacier, and fantasized about becoming an alpine guide too. On our return to the refuge I would imitate my teacher: I tried to talk like him (very little), walk like him (lightly, almost as if weightless), and to adopt the same attitude as his when faced with dangers such as being on the rock face in a rainstorm (whistling). I had learned from him so well that once, when he was in training for the Himalayas, he had come to ask me to race with him—just the two of us, up to a height of thirteen thousand feet and back again in only a few hours. With just a rope, the coordination of our steps, and no further need to ask or give instructions. Thirteen thousand feet was easily done, after all. We had almost immediately disappeared into the clouds, and had seen nothing further until the evening, just the amorphous white of the ice and mist—and yet it was the most beautiful memory that I cherished of him, of our private Himalaya.

That must have been the last time that we went mountaineering together: afterward I was drawn to other places, and was guided by other teachers. Yet none of them would inspire in me the unconditional trust I gave to Renzo. Now fifteen years had passed, and I wondered whether he ever asked himself what had become of me: who knows what he would have thought if he'd known that I was there on the other side, just beyond the hill, playing at being a hermit in a hut. If truth be told, he was one of the reasons why I had ended up there.

I shared these thoughts with Remigio, who I found easy to talk to. From the outset we had established between us a sense of familiarity—from the day of the books and the snow—and it had grown in the dust of haymaking. We went back and forth from the fields, with him driving the tractor and me sitting in the rickety trailer. In the hayloft we would fling the bales at each other and pile them in stacks about a dozen feet high. One evening after work he invited me around to his place for a drink of the kind that his mother prohibited, and in the living room I was surprised to find a typewriter. It was a well-kept bygone. There was a sheet of paper loaded, and on the sheet of paper there was a single line: *I wonder if I'll be able to write as before.* I was disconcerted by the phrase: whatever did that mountain man have to do with writing? Afterward it disturbed me more deeply, since I was familiar with such doubts myself: I had not written for months, and feared that I would never do so again. When I asked him to explain its meaning, Remigio said that the sheet of paper had been there for twenty years: it dated back to the period when his father died, and he had not touched the typewriter since.

I began to listen with the respect that you feel when entering into other people's lives, the same sense of awe. Remigio's father had been a hunter, a builder of houses, and a storyteller. He would take him to the woods when he was a child, to set traps for animals, and had taught him to identify in the snow the tracks of foxes, marmots, and ermine. Years later he had taken him on as a laborer on the building sites, inducting him into the art of raising walls. They had been very close—Remigio was an only son, and there were no other young men in the village—until their relationship had been ruined by alcohol. At a certain point that affectionate and outgoing man had started to drink hard—so hard that he had fallen seriously ill. His character changed, or perhaps it was his son who had become reserved and bad-tempered with age, and that there was nothing to be done with such a drunken father but to argue. Accompanying him in and out of the hospital, he had watched him being slowly destroyed—and it had fallen to him, in the end, to find his father in the field where he had gone to die. He could never forgive himself that their last words had been words of anger.

Now what remained of his father was his hunting trophies, sinister custodians of the room in which we were talking: the hooves of a chamois turned into coat hooks, a pair of ibex horns mounted on a wooden plaque, stuffed specimens of martens and ermine. The feathers of an eagle that his father had shot for a challenge, and that in its death agony had clutched his arm until Remigio had rushed over to get the bird off him, using all his strength to break her talons. From that moment on, hunting was repulsive to him. The *passion*, as hunters call it, had not been bequeathed to him along with the shotguns.

But there was another legacy that he did preserve. Shortly before his death his father had left him the ruins of a hut in the middle of a meadow. A small stable below, above it a single room, a roof with warped and skewed shingles made of larch, and walls blackened by smoke and encrusted with dung. He had included no words of explanation along with this mysterious gift. Then he had died. Years later, Remigio had discovered its meaning for himself—and to assuage his feelings of guilt he had spent two long summers renovating the building. He had decided to work alone, without assistance from builders or machinery, excavating the earth with only the power of a pickax, raising the beams on a ramp of planks, with a rope and a tractor. They were from trees that he had cut down himself in the woods, choosing them with the care that he used on every other detail: every piece of wood, every nail, every stone of the house, so that the work was done perfectly, as his father, the bricklayer, had taught him. Then he had finished it, spending just one night under its roof before understanding that he would never live there. There were too many presences between its four walls to sleep well at night. So he had rented it out. Better to leave the bewitched place to someone who knew nothing about it. Ten years later I had turned up, looking for a place to be alone in—and this was the story I had strayed into, hoping to find how to write again.

Goats

In the summer the wild animals had all disappeared. It was the fault of the people who had begun to hit the mountain tracks, pushing them into ever more remote areas. I encountered these people every day around my house, and they seemed blind and deaf to the landscape through which they were moving, making so much noise that I could hear them long before they came into view. Even their chemically produced scents seemed to strike me from a distance. Is it just me, I asked myself, who has problems with the rest of humanity? Or is it they who don't know how to walk the earth without invading it? They would burst into the woods with a riot of smells, colors, noise. And the woodland animals naturally reacted by making themselves scarce.

I was missing my neighbors: the hares, foxes, and deer. So one morning I got up at six, gulped down a single cup of coffee, and set out for a long walk. No rucksack, flask, or boots—just a stick and shoes, light as the wind. After three months up there I felt in great shape. I left behind the wood and the first pastures, Gabriele's lodge and the marmots' clearings, the abandoned and crumbling villages. I stopped at the stream to drink, then sped to get beyond the high pastures too, so that by seven I had in front of me nothing but scree, the small lakes of the thaw, and residual snow. I breathed the pure morning air just before the sun rose from behind the crests and the day broke in earnest. Nobody seemed to have come before me.

On the scree I slowed down, careful not to noisily dislodge any stones. Arriving at the ridge I had a stroke of luck: I must have been downwind, or perhaps I already reeked of goat myself, but either way I saw two chamois standing on a small snowfield. I had surprised them in the midst of one of their secret games. All around the scree was warming up, the snow reduced to small, frozen, and glittering patches— and the chamois were rolling about on their bellies, backs, and flanks, delighting in this vestige of winter. They would slide down for a bit, then get up and clamber back to the top of the snowfield. They carried on in this way until, ears suddenly pricked, one of them sensed danger. I hid between the rocks and tried not to move, but something had already spooked them. The more cautious of the two was the first to leave, the other one hesitating before following, as if with regret at the interruption of their game—before disappearing into the scree with a few elegant bounds.

I continued to climb: who was going to stop me now? Now I was on the ridge between the two valleys of my life, and I was walking on slabs of broken rock fractured by ice, and on that unbelievably soft moss that grows at ten thousand feet. On one side of the watershed, that of adulthood, the sky was clear and of such an intense blue that it seemed to have mass and volume. On the side of childhood, puffs of clouds were rising and curled up to and dissolved at my feet. Over there I had spent twenty years, over here the last few months: two valleys gouged by two rivers, and two rivers born from the same mountain. It was the mountain which I now had before my eyes, Monte Rosa, that united my present and my past.

Then I saw some dark shapes, figures moving on the jagged rock. It was a small herd of male ibex. Less cautious than chamois, they have not been hunted for a century and have ceased to fear man. They stay up there on the crests and pinnacles because they love to survey their kingdom from on high, in the wind and the blinding light. The herd consisted of a majestic alpha male that had eased itself down and assumed on a ledge the solemn pose of a leader, four restless young bucks that were goading each other, and a venerable animal so old and tired that he moved only with painful difficulty. His coat was mangy, the weight of his horns such that he could no longer support it, forcing him to keep his neck bent toward the ground. As soon as I was spotted, the leader of the group stood up and placed himself between the rest of the herd and me. He was staring at me, emitting a battle cry like a sustained F blown from full lungs. He had horns that were three feet long, and powerful muscles to carry them: it would have taken him very little effort to thrust me out of his territory, if not to say out of this world altogether. But I was trying to make him see that I had come in peace. The young males jumped onto a rock, finding safety behind him, while the older one had to take a circuitous route to join them. I sat down on the ground and remained still for a minute, until the alpha male concluded that I was a tedious adversary, and gave one last snort before commencing to graze on the moss that carpeted the rocks. In training for the mating season, two of the youngsters began to butt each other with their horns: they raised themselves up on their back legs before letting themselves fall upon their rival, using all their weight to lend power to their blows and producing with their horns a blunt *tock*, like the sound of two rocks being knocked together. By now the old buck was the only one paying me any attention: he had squatted down in front of me, nine or ten feet away, and scrutinized me while ruminating, scratching his back occasionally with his horns. I counted around fifteen knots in them: fifteen years spent wandering the mountains, without enemies and without ever descending to the valley. What a wonderful life, I thought. Who knows whether this would be his last summer, or whether he would be able to overcome his aches and pains and survive another winter. Who knows what kind of questions he was asking about me.

Then I looked down through the clear air of eight in the morning. I could see clearly the roads at the bottom of the valley, where the sun would not reach for another few hours yet. That shadowy world had the appearance of an alien planet: with the cars coming and going between villages that had sprawled out of all proportion, the neighborhoods of condominiums and chalets spreading like city suburbs. And then the quarries of sand and gravel in the riverbeds, the pistes that cut swathes through the woods, the parking lots at the bottom of the skiing developments, building sites everywhere. An industrious and invasive species, wholly dedicated to eroding, leveling, colonizing: this is what humanity looked like from the vantage point of the mountain crests, where to live it was sufficient to graze a little grass and lie down in the sun. I observed the house in which I had been a child, or rather the apartment complex that was rising where it had once been. The house of my childhood had ceased to exist some time ago, and this seemed only right. A

crane was positioned next to a silo of cement in the courtyard, making me wonder what had happened to the large
wild cherry tree that used to be there. My gaze met that of
the old buck's again, and this time I felt I knew clearly what
he was thinking. Sorry, I felt like replying.

I went down in no hurry that morning, feeling hostile toward the place I was going back to. The hut, my collection
of finds, the unused notebooks, the books. A small garret
room so full of me, while outside the mountain offered itself, unexplored, in every direction. What did I need a house
for? I would like to have followed the example of the shepherds of times past, who would wander from one pasture
to another, stopping to sleep in the shelters provided by the
rocks. I would sometimes come across these in my explorations: protruding boulders at the base of which the ground
had been cleared and sometimes enclosed with a drystone
wall. They had a name for these in the local dialect, which
I had heard uttered by Remigio while we were haymaking.
What is a *barma*? I'd asked him. A rock giving shelter when
it rains, he'd replied.

Down at the hut it was midday, and a small family had
spread a blanket on the grass in front of it. Two children
were splashing each other in the fountain, the mother had

taken out bags and containers, the father gave me the once-over with the kind of surly stare that men exchange when there is territory or family to defend. It's possible that I was looking at him that way too.

Excuse me, is this private property? his wife asked me, rather more courteously.

No, no, I said, it's for everyone, please stay.

Once inside I unhooked the rucksack from the nail on which it was hanging, stuffed a few items of clothing inside together with a waterproof ground sheet, a sleeping bag, a flask of wine, all the tins I had in the kitchen, and a lighter, a knife, strips of newspaper, a torch, two hooks, a pen, and a notebook. I wanted to push myself beyond the area I was familiar with, to discover what lay two or three days' walking distance from there. I was setting off with that load—yet shutting the door behind me it seemed as if I was freeing myself of a burden. The burden, as usual, could be the hut or the people who in my eyes had profaned it, but it was much more likely that it was myself. What do we run from when we run away from home? So long, said the wild boy to the domestic double of himself, then turned his back on him and took the rising path.

Bivouacking

Down the slope that had been engulfed by a landslide my boots sank into the soft earth: a grayish, viscous paste, like fresh malt, making each step laborious. I mounted an uprooted trunk and balanced along its length to cross a chaos of dislodged rocks, rivulets of muddy water, and enormous clods flung around as in the aftermath of an explosion—resting precariously here on the brink of a boulder or stuck there in a crack in the earth, insisting on putting forth flowers even in these unnatural positions. Up above, a wide, dark strip showed where the mountain had split. It was damp and rotten rock face, with larch roots that stuck out halfway up and could not hold it together. Of wildlife there was no trace: not a whistle of alarm, no sudden going to ground as I passed by. It was as if they had migrated en masse from the site of that disaster. Even the birds were silent, leaving only the gurgle of a subterranean stream to be carried through the air. I felt relieved when at last I got beyond the final debris, found a trace of the path that turned to the left, and leaving behind the landslide, started to climb again.

I had the idea of spending the night on the shore of a lake, warming myself next to a fire and gazing at the August night sky, but it was not to be: that was a summer of rain, and when I arrived there I could feel the storm approaching. A front of dark, swollen clouds was thundering several miles away in the valley, above the village I had left just a few hours ago. Two fishermen were busying themselves putting up a small Canadian-style tent in the wind. The wind arrived in furious squalls, crenellating the surface of the lake and pushing the clouds toward us, so I headed in the direction of a cluster of ruined buildings, hoping to find shelter there. There was a hut less dilapidated than the rest: the walls were managing to stay upright if skewed, and a sheet of corrugated iron had been placed on the roof. I thought to myself that if somebody was still using it there would be a padlock somewhere, or even a proper lock on the door. But I could see no keyhole. The door was completely warped and wedged in place by sheer force. I tried pushing against it with my hands, felt that it was giving way, and shoved it with my shoulder, flinging it wide open.

My eyes were slow to adjust to the dark. Outside, the rain was beginning to drum on the corrugated metal. Inside, there were no windows, but a gap between the walls and the roof allowed a little light to permeate. The hearth was at the center of the room: four flat stones to contain the brazier, in the corner the revolving hook to hang the cauldron from. Then a wooden shelf with an oil lamp, a few empty bottles, some candle ends, a toy gun. What was a toy gun doing there? It was a replica revolver, badly broken and held together with Scotch tape. Seeing it, I was reminded of the shepherds' children I had seen in the mountains when I was small: filthy, diffident, behaving like adults when they looked after their cows—and I tried to imagine what they got up to when there was nobody around to see them. I also found a sliver of mirror and a dirty bowl, two metal cups and a foul, ripped-open mattress. It must have been the mice who had shredded it, I thought, because the floor was littered with balls of dirty wool as well as fragments of broken bottles, hay, and who knows what else. Fortunately, there wasn't enough light to reveal it. The storm was now making a deafening racket; I cleared a corner of the floor as best I could to spread out my sleeping bag, then sat down and opened my rucksack.

A piece of black bread, a tin of meat, two tomatoes, and a little wine would make up that evening's menu. Pinned down by all that rain, dinner was my only distraction—so I tried to make it last for as long as possible, chewing the bread slowly and taking small sips of the wine. But then the storm relented. I found some dry wood in another corner of the room and lit a fire outside, a few feet from the hut, because I feared that I would be smoked if I used the fireplace. When the rain started again it was already a lively bonfire. Sitting in the doorway I managed to keep dry and have a little light to read by, so I spent the evening in the company of a book by Primo Levi, *The Periodic Table*, an autobiography in the form of short stories. Above me towered the mountain that I would have to overcome the next day: every so often I would raise my eyes to study it, until it became too dark to see anything at all.

I went inside, lit the candle stubs, and continued reading in the sleeping bag. In "Iron," the fourth story in the book, Levi remembers his friendship with Sandro Delmastro, whom he had met in 1938 in the chemistry department at the University of Turin. It was a meeting between two marginalized individuals: Levi had just become one on account of Mussolini's racial laws (the son of middle-class Turinese parents, he was shocked and scared by the caution with which his peers suddenly regarded him); Sandro had always been one, due to his shoes and clothes, his hands and his way of walking, the language and the general way of doing things that he had brought down with him from the mountains near Ivrea in order to study in the city. A Jewish youth and a man of the mountains: between them there was a mutual recognition, and they began to help each other. Primo helped Sandro with the chemistry that was in the textbooks, convinced that therein was to be found the key to the mystery of matter; Sandro would take Primo to touch that very matter with his own hands, and to come to understand the mystery through rocks, streams, wind, and snow. In the mountains, in those increasingly tenebrous days that preceded "Europe's darkest hour," they had forged their friendship and enjoyed their last moments of freedom.

He would drag me on exhausting canters through the fresh snow, far from any trace of humanity, following itineraries that he seemed to intuit like a primitive. In the summer, from refuge to refuge, getting drunk on sunshine, exertion and wind, and sanding smooth the skin of our fingertips on the rock that no human hand had touched before. But not on the famous peaks, nor in pursuit of a memorable exploit; these things did not matter to him at all. What he cared about was to know his own limits, to challenge and to improve himself. And more obscurely, he felt the need to prepare himself (and to prepare me as well) for an iron future that was getting closer with each passing month.

To see Sandro in the mountains helped me to be reconciled with the world, to forget the nightmare that was looming over Europe. It was a place that belonged to him, that he had been made for, like the marmots whose whistles and calls he imitated: in the mountains he became happy, with a quiet and infectious happiness, like the turning on of a light. He aroused in me a new sense of communion with the earth and sky, in which my need for freedom, the fullness of my strength, and that hunger to understand the nature of things that had compelled me towards chemistry all flowed together.

Numerous times during the night the rain stopped and started again. I too found myself constantly falling asleep and then waking again. For certain brief moments, in that confused overlapping of states of consciousness, I dreamed that presences were moving around me in the hut. The ghost of a solitary shepherd perhaps, or of two youths who had preceded me by about seventy years. Primo and Sandro might have passed by this very place on one of their forays:

I was wandering in the same mountains they had tramped through. One day they had taken a wrong turn and had become lost, with Primo suggesting they turn back and Sandro adamant in his desire to proceed. "The worst that can happen," he remarked enigmatically, "is that we'll taste bear meat." Night had fallen, and the two friends had resigned themselves to spending it in the open air, huddled together, teeth chattering, staring at the moon and a sky "of tattered clouds." At first light they had descended toward the refuge, stumbling with cold and tiredness.

I too got up when the sky began to pale. It must have been five in the morning. I could not bear to spend a moment longer turning from side to side on the floor, avoiding the broken glass and the water that was coming down from the roof, thinking how time managed to contract and expand; how a whole year could fly past in the blink of an eye and one night could seem never-ending. I rolled up my sleeping bag and packed my rucksack again, laced my boots, and left the newspaper with which I had lit the fire, thinking that sooner or later it would be needed by someone else. Then I said farewell to the hut that had given me shelter, pulled the door shut behind me, and took a deep breath.

Outside, the air was damp and cold. I felt racked with pains and still tired from the night before, but I knew that this feeling would vanish in the course of my walk. I tried not to fixate on the word *coffee*. I stopped by a small stream, brushed my teeth, and washed my face and neck until I was fully awake. The morning was becoming clear, with the lake still in shadow about six hundred and fifty feet below me and the mountain summit three thousand feet above already lit by the sun. Patches of grayish snow lingered on the black rock, but beyond it there was a new whiteness, sparkling and almost silver-tinted, striating the rock walls, inscribing edges and folds as if marked out with chalk. I thought that up there it might have snowed, but I had never seen the snow delineated with such clear-cut lines. I would discover later that it was not snow but ice—the hail that in the night had accumulated in cracks and on ledges, and that in the sunlight formed glittering veins. Ahead were at least two hours on the scree before I could get up there to gawp, amazed, at the ice between my fingers. So I lowered my head, mule-like, hitched my thumbs into the straps of my rucksack, and asked my trusty legs to get back to work.

And to the innkeeper, who asked us while sniggering how we had got on and glanced at our dazed faces, we replied defiantly that we'd had an excellent outing. We paid the bill and left with dignity. This was it, the *bear meat*: and now that so many years have passed, I regret that I did not eat more of it, because of all the good things which life has afforded me, nothing comes close to the flavor of that flesh, which is the flavor of being strong and free—free to make mistakes, the master of one's own destiny.

Refuge

No matter how early I got up, in the refuge there was always someone who had risen before me. My window faced east, toward a chain of black mountains from which dawn arrived at six in the morning, illuminating the wall in front of my bed and tingeing the room orange and gold. I would open my eyes in that sudden light, the sleeping bag reduced to a tangle of disturbed dreams. It was the smell of the fire that reminded me where I was. Beechwood, with a scent quite unlike the larch I used at home. The stove kept burning it all day but would barely warm the kitchen. During that rainy August we always gathered together there: on the stove we prepared coffee, cooked, hung out our laundry to dry, toasted the pistachios we had found one day, damp and who knows how old, in the bottom of a cupboard in the pantry.

It was an antique refuge, built in the nineteenth century

to provide shelter for the emigrants who returned home in winter. It was located at an elevation of eight thousand feet, on the border pass between two valleys—one plunged westward, from where I had come, the other stretched more gently east, toward the summits and the valleys I could see from my bedroom, along an ancient track for men and goods that had now fallen into disuse. The age of mules having become obsolete, the mountain was off all the routes, surrounded as it was by others regarded by mountaineers as lacking nobility, and by ordinary walkers as too inaccessible. Instead the refuge was perfect for me, because that world had all the wildness I could desire: made of broken rock, crests, snowfields, and with no one else around.

I had stopped over to sleep the night and then in the morning had one of my ideas. With all the nerve that I could muster I had asked its two keepers if I could lodge there in exchange for work, given that I was tired of wandering around: I liked the place but did not have the money to cover many days' board and lodging. They had given me a peculiar look. I was the only guest that night, and the refuge hardly seemed to be a flourishing business. But they had consulted each other, and perhaps they had understood something of what I was not saying. We were all of an age, around thirty. In the end they had replied that there was no work available, but that I could stay with them anyway for as long as I liked, free of charge, if I was prepared to share that life. I could hardly have asked for more.

In the space in front of the refuge an Italian flag flew. Although it was replaced every year in June, the wind would little by little tatter and fade it during the summer, so the condition of that flag became a clock with which to measure the time I spent up there. By the time I arrived the band of red had almost gone, and you could barely make out a frayed trace of it against the sky. When I left, there was half of the white band left—a stump of the nation that well expressed the spirit of the mountain pass, our life on a brink.

Of the two keepers, Andrea was the earlier riser, and the one I would get on with best. By the time I came down he'd already lit the stove, set up breakfast, washed the dishes from the previous night, and was smoking and watching films on his mobile, or scanning through profiles of girls on the Web. He always sat in the same place at the table, near the window wet with condensation. Toward eleven he shifted from coffee to wine diluted with water, or Pernod and water instead, or white wine and Campari, rolling cigarettes with golden Virginia, inviting me to have a drink and showing me the tourists—English, female—that he'd taught to ski during the winter. Now they were on a beach somewhere, posting photos of themselves in swimwear. They looked like mermaids from infinitely far-off seas. Above us it rained daily, and sometimes the rain became a mush that was almost snow—and when it didn't rain or snow, a freezing wind gusted that beat me back as soon as I poked my nose outside. The only flesh and blood female was an athlete who was in training for mountain racing: through the binoculars we would watch her as she climbed up the track, commenting on the way she looked and hoping that at least once she would stop for a coffee. But she would reach the pass, touch the wall of the refuge, turn on her heels, and head back down again, as fleeting as every other glimpse of beauty. To watch her going was even more alluring, though in a much more melancholy way, than to see her coming up.

Davide slept until late, and was the last one to come down to the kitchen—but from that point he was constantly on the go. Every other day he kneaded the dough that he baked in the oven of the stove. He kept the accounts, answered the phone, and was the one who greeted the guests, given that Andrea preferred to stay in the kitchen and speak as little as possible. Davide had many more ideas than he ever got to put into action. Investments, parties, schemes to improve the efficiency of the refuge. If he found himself at a loose end, he would grab a chisel from the windowsill and begin whittling a handle for a knife. He would say that he could never draw anything symmetrical. He was convinced that there was something inside him that was at war with symmetry, perhaps on account of the cheekbone that he had fractured years ago, and that had so marked his features. Sitting there on rainy days he talked nonstop. It was like having the radio on.

I had taken over the kitchen. Sifting through the pantry, I had salvaged rice, pulses, flour, tomato sauce, tins of tuna fish, anchovies, and olives. There were sacks of enough onions and potatoes to last until September. The butter, eggs, and cheese were sourced from an alpeggio just down from us, and this was all I had to invent our daily meals from.

Apart from the limited diet and the chronic absence of women, our main problem was the electricity supply. There wasn't enough sun to feed the panels, the wind turbine was still only a dream in Davide's head, and the gas had to be rationed. So when guests arrived we turned on the generator, otherwise the afternoon meant getting gradually accustomed to the dark. Sitting at the head of the table, I read aloud the poems of Antonia Pozzi, and a book that I had found in the refuge, the story of an ex-soldier of the Napoleonic era who had lived up there summer and winter for forty years, tasked with clearing the track after each snowfall, ringing the fog bell, keeping the stove alight for any new arrival. A century and a half later we were not leading such a different life there. Toward six, by moving to the window, I managed to catch on the pages a little of that milky glow, just enough to make out the words printed there. Later we lit a candle, and when that was finished it was time for bed.

I was surprised that these men had welcomed me so naturally, but also felt that I understood why they'd done so. We had been pushed up there by the same needs, and it hadn't taken us long to recognize each other. In bed I would place two blankets on top of my sleeping bag. I would get into it in total darkness. I slept in clothes that were redolent of onion soup, stew left to cook for hours, damp wool, and woodsmoke—the smell that I would keep for a long time, since it was the fragrance of home.

It was easy to lose track of the passing days. Outside the window, a uniform whiteness reigned—the same from morning till night. Only at dawn did I happen to catch sight of the sea of clouds from above, just as if our world was separated from the one below, the one bright and clear, the other rain-sodden and gloomy. But shortly the tide would rise, swallowing the woods, the meadows, the scree, eventually lapping against the final slope before engulfing us as well. Closed in the kitchen, we would listen to the flag's metal cable banging against the flagpole, and that clinking was the music of the mountain, along with the whistles of marmots, the creaking of shutters in the wind, the crackling of the stove, the guitar occasionally taken up by Davide or Andrea, even though neither one of them really knew how to play.

Occasionally someone would turn up. Only a couple at a time, and we could spot them from above with our binoculars. Andrea called them *the ephemeral ones*. Davide would greet them at the door, serve them a plate of polenta and sausage and a glass of wine before rejoining us in the kitchen. We kept our distance, not because we disliked visitors but because those people belonged to the world below and brought news of it with them, news that we did not want to receive. We were fine without it. When the ephemerals took off we would watch them receding, becoming ever smaller before finally vanishing round a bend in the path, giving us a comforting sense of once more being alone.

A Good Bottle

One morning a gap opened in the cloud cover. Among the stuff in the refuge I had found a fishing rod, so I asked Davide and Andrea where I might use it.

At the lake that isn't there, they said.

Why is it called that?

Because sometimes you find it, and sometimes not.

And are there any trout in it?

If you can find the lake, then maybe you'll also find the trout.

They pointed to a road that passed along the line of the watershed and then crossed it westward, in the middle of the scree, always keeping to the higher ground. Whether the lake was there or not, after days on end shut in the refuge I was desperate to stretch my legs, so I packed the fishing rod into my rucksack and set off. At a good pace I passed the flag and reached the rock where Davide and

Andrea had carved their initials, together with those of a friend of theirs who was no longer alive, under a small cross. On the crest I disturbed some chamois and deviated from the path in order to chase them, until I saw them disappear down the frozen wake gouged by an avalanche. I had not set foot on snow for weeks and decided to throw myself down too. I slipped, fell, got back up again, laughed out loud to myself, and gave in to the sudden urge to shout. I remembered it being the case all the way back to my childhood, this transformation that the mountain provoked in me: this joy in having a body, the sense of harmony that you rediscover moving in its element, this freedom to run and jump and scramble as if your hands and feet were moving of their own accord and it was really impossible to come to any harm. At this point I possessed a body without age—no longer the one that, a few winters ago, I had begun to feel growing old.

The mysterious lake really did exist. I could understand how it had got its name: sunk between massive boulders shaped by glaciers, at an altitude of nine thousand feet, you could easily pass by its black water without noticing the presence of the lake. I caught a few grasshoppers in the sparse grass up there and put them into a jar to use as bait. Fishing . . . I had only gone fishing a few times in my life, but then perhaps the trout in that lake had only seen a few fishermen: casting my line near the shore I caught three small ones, not much longer than the width of my palm. The fourth time I threw it farther out. I managed to catch a glimpse of a large moving shadow, felt a tug, and pulled in response—only to instantly lose both catch and rod to the lake. Here was the fish that was not, I thought. Being a novice, I had not brought along any backup equipment, and in any case the sky was becoming overcast again and I decided to head back.

Once on the ridge again I had a vision: I was in the midst of clouds, and a glimmer of sun suddenly appeared behind me. The sun projected a circular rainbow onto the clouds, and in the middle of this circle there was the shadow of a man. It took me a while to understand that it was me. I was tall and thin, with extremely long legs and arms that I waved in order to greet that double of myself, an alien suffused with light. The spectacle did not last long because almost immediately the sun dimmed and the air became electric. Right, I told myself, so now I'm about to have a shower. Inside the rucksack I had the spoils of my fishing trip, and during the run back I enumerated to myself all the recipes that I could imagine: baked trout, trout fried in lard, fillets of trout, soused trout, trout sautéed with local butter and wild thyme. I wanted to prepare a good lunch for my friends. When our half flag emerged from the fog, the first drops were already falling; in front of the refuge I opened the jar with the bait and freed the remaining grasshoppers before going inside.

With Andrea I shared my mornings, and something else besides. We were too similar not to recognize our similarity, and not to be a little unsettled by it, as when passing a shop window you are reflected in it, only realizing after a slight delay that it is you. Ours was not a physical resemblance, but one of personality, that is to say the similar ways we both were with ourselves and with others, a certain tendency toward idealism and a skin that was too thin for the rough and tumble of relationships, consequently leading us to have had great enthusiasms and great retreats from them. Silence and solitude provided a good temporary hiding place. Wine also helped, for as long as it did not become a problem. I already knew these things about myself, but it was the first time that I had seen them so clearly delineated in someone else. That it should happen up there, inside an old refuge, on the borderline between two valleys, gave our meeting the feeling of something prearranged. It could not last long, because nobody can endure the company of another self for long, or at least the two of us could not.

He was born into the trade, that is to say he was the son

of a caretaker of an alpine refuge, and the grandson of a mountain man he'd spent summers with in an alpeggio as a child. As a grown-up he had adapted to the times: in the winter he was a ski instructor in a French resort (with discos and pubs) at the foot of the slopes, and in this way he earned enough to live off of for the rest of the year. The refuge was not a job but a way of staying far away from the village that he had begun to feel was dangerous, of hiding in the mountains where instead, at least for a little while, he felt that he was safe. What these dangers in the valley were, it was not necessary to say. Better to take three months caretaking a refuge where nobody came.

He was secure, but not happy. When our friendship was developed enough to confide in each other he told me that he couldn't stand being in the mountains any longer. What do you mean? I said, convinced that the connection we had was based on an elective affinity for high altitudes. I was confusing roots with vocation—or perhaps Andrea, who had been born there, felt the same need as I did to freely choose his own place in the world: he wanted to leave for warmer climes, to Greece or to Sicily. He told me about the trips he used to go on in the fall, between the season of the refuge and the start of the skiing, on some beach in the south with the sun, white wine, the fish, the lemons. There was a girl included in these voyages to the happy isles. Andrea was intending to extract enough money from the wealthy American skiers that hired him in the winter to buy a little house by the sea with her—and to kiss goodbye to the refuge, the snow, and everything else besides. Something told me that he would succeed in doing this.

There was a peak nearby that belonged to him, to such an extent that it bore the name of his family, and it was the only one we climbed together. It happened just before my departure. That evening other friends from the village came and stayed overnight, and in the morning Davide put up a sign with the message GONE TO THE MOUNTAIN, then we shut the door of the refuge and followed the usual track. There are those who like to walk in groups, and those who almost without meaning to find themselves immediately on their own: I was drawn by the crest that I had already begun to explore, and headed for it. I saw that Andrea was also setting off below, along a road, disappearing between boulders among which he moved lightly, the two of us leaving the path to friends who walk in line. The crest soon began to demand my undivided attention. I got beyond the frozen avalanche I had gone down by the first time, and past the point from which I could see the lake that wasn't there from above, obstinately insisting on keeping to the brink rather than taking one of the chamois tracks, easier prospects, that started on either side. In a few places I was obliged to use my hands, at first only to gain a hold and then to pull myself up, until I found myself astride the rock, with two smooth rock faces beneath my feet, asking myself whether I was not doing something idiotic. Then the climb became easier, a wide spine of wobbly flat slabs, almost a game of hopscotch choosing which rock to jump on. There was one last ledge beneath the summit, and it was there that I met up again with Andrea: he was going up a long gorge by himself and we came together by chance where the two ways crossed. We were more amused than annoyed by this, since some distance apart and without either of us watching what the other was doing, we had managed to keep exactly the same pace: a rare coincidence that neither of us felt the need to mention.

He, however, had the foresight to bring a bottle, whereas I had not. He extracted it from his rucksack and uncorked it on the summit that shared his name, while the others caught up. We'd shared a few drinks together, but the last was the best: we wrote our names and the date in the summit book, and I was pleased that in a small notebook hidden at almost ten thousand feet they were inscribed close together. They were not carved into the rock, but for a few years up there the mountain would preserve them.

Mists. And the thud of stones
in the canals. Voices of water
come down from the snowfields
of the night.

You stretch a blanket for me
on the straw mat:
with your rough hands
you cover my shoulders, lightly,
lest I catch cold.

I think
of the great mystery that lives
within you, beyond your slow
gesture; about the meaning
of this our human brotherhood
without words, amongst the immense rocks
of the mountains.
And perhaps there are more stars
And secrets and unfathomable ways
between us, in the silence,
than in the whole of the sky stretching out
on the other side of the mist.

Antonia Pozzi, "Refuge"

Crying

It had been building for some time, and of all the unfortunate places it could have happened, I burst into tears, in the end, in the middle of one of the scree slopes that I loved so much. For almost an hour I had gradually been getting slower: I would climb a few paces, stop, bend down to catch my breath, look up toward the outline of the ridge and feel as if I had not advanced by even a single foot. How many had I already got over like this? Five or six massive rocky walls, judging from the route, in the hope that on the other side there would be a way of getting down without killing myself. Things had not always gone well for me. Twice I'd reached the top only to find myself looking out over a precipice, and consequently had to retreat and try to cross at another point instead. I had started to feel tired several hours ago, and now I was practically exhausted—with the rucksack straps gnawing into my shoulders and a feeling of nausea brought on by fatigue, altitude, and a discomfort that I had not experienced since childhood. It was in this frame of mind that I was confronted by a section even more difficult than anything I'd tackled so far. When I placed my hand on the rock face and tried to climb, I discovered that I had lost all agility. I slipped from a hold and landed lower down, sat without meaning to on a large flat stone. The pain registered soon enough. A lacerating pain in my hip and half-flayed leg, though it seemed that nothing had been broken. I lay down on the stone, using the rucksack as a backrest. It was then that I felt a sob rising in my throat, my eyes misting. Go on, cry, I thought, no one can see you. Lying on that stone I began to sob because I was tired, because I missed the others, and because I had no idea where I was.

Already, at the height of August, summer was declining toward the precocious mountain fall. I had left the refuge early in the morning, but I wasn't at all happy to be going away—so for the return journey I had decided to change route. It would be less melancholy, I thought, if I was to convert my farewell into an adventure. There was a village some six miles away, where when they celebrated their patron saint the shepherds shared the festivities with whoever went up there. In order to arrive there, according to the map, I would have needed to go down three thousand feet and then climb back up another thousand in a parallel gorge, but I had convinced myself that I could get there by remaining at altitude, finding a way of circumventing the mountain. Looking for shortcuts is a predictable enough way of getting into trouble. I had begun to cross a long detrital escarpment, with only the occasional tuft of grass or patch of juniper or rhododendrons, and the last frozen snow in the gullies. Time was its usual enigma. I would spend a long while enveloped in clouds that every so often cleared to let me study the way ahead. On my right I had a chain of peaks, and from each one an escarpment descended: the only thing was, I didn't know how many there were, nor what difficulties they concealed. To work out where to cross I watched some chamois. I made out their movements from below, followed their footsteps on the ridges and the short, beaten tracks: vertiginous routes that cut the flanks of the mountain like high-altitude pistes, and which stopped abruptly where the chamois dispersed. So I was struggling up a slope, asking myself what could be on the other side, hoping for a plateau or a basin, only to get to the top of the crest and discover that I had another uneven descent in front of me, more uneven scree, another climb similar to the one I had just completed.

It was penance for my sin of arrogance. Hours later,

stretched out sobbing on that boulder, I could still see no end in sight.

Now I was watching the sky, envying the clouds that moved effortlessly from one valley to the next. I felt stupid, arrogant, dragged up there by an inane game: to get lost so as to see whether I was capable of finding the road again, escaping far away from people to find out whether somebody missed me. I had gone to the mountains with the idea that, if I stuck at it for long enough, at a certain point I would become transformed into someone else, and the transformation would be irreversible. In the event my old self was coming out in even more exaggerated ways. I had learned how to chop wood, to light a fire in a rainstorm, to hoe and plant a vegetable garden, to milk a cow, and to stack bales of hay; but I had not learned how to be alone—the only true aim, ultimately, of any hermit-like retreat. In this respect I felt exactly the same as on the day that I'd arrived. The skin on my hands had become thicker, my body had become sturdier and more resilient, but my spirit had not been toughened or reinforced: it remained as sickly and frail as ever. More than a hut in the woods, solitude resembled a house of mirrors; everywhere I looked I found myself reflected: distorted, grotesque, multiplied an infinite number of times. I could free myself of everything except him. Which is why, stretched out on that flat stone, I decided that my experiment had been a complete failure.

While I was feeling sorry for myself I saw an eagle circling directly above me. It was describing ever narrower circles, as if it was targeting something, and I instinctively suspected that I was the prey. I was lying down, motionless, and as far as the eagle was concerned I might well be dead already. If I had been dead, I thought, she would have overcome all inhibitions and flown down to feast. I had come across chamois and ibex before that had been filleted to the bone: their skeletons saddened me, but the thought that they had provided a meal for another creature was consoling. Given the choice, I too would like to have such an ending.

Then I got up. Immediately the eagle regained height and moved away. I adjusted the straps of the rucksack, sealed the clasp of the belt around my waist. The injury I had was not too painful, and I knew that I still had some energy left. I detoured around the point at which I'd fallen and began to climb again with the same rhythm as before: two steps and a pause, two steps and a pause, without looking up any more, focusing only on where to place my feet.

I did not realize that I was at the top of the ridge until I'd actually reached it, and from up there I could make out the village I was searching for. Ten or so sheltered huts, two or three hundred yards below me, with animals grazing in the surrounding fields. There was a vast copper cauldron on an open fire, and a man tending it. In front of a small white chapel a modest crowd had gathered, from which a song arose that somebody was accompanying with a trumpet. I don't believe I'd ever been so happy before to see a mass and to hear church music. I took off my rucksack, lay down, and closed my eyes again, this time to enjoy the music in the sunshine.

AUTUMN

Season of Writing

Return

In the afternoon I was back in the hut. From a distance it seemed to be hiding between the trees, popping out in front of me as sometimes happens with people, when you turn a corner and bump into someone who'd been a friend in the past but wasn't any longer, and you don't know whether to embrace him or pass by with your eyes averted. I felt like this about the hut. An ibex skull that I'd found in June and called *the god of Fontane* was still surveying his kingdom from the windowsill. The meadows were only a little yellower, and the bowl I used for the dogs was lying upside down in the grass. Well at least they must have missed me a little, I thought. And the vegetable garden had felt my absence even more: invaded by weeds and devastated by some calf in search of a salad. His hoofprints were still visible in the soft soil. Rather more courteously, I took off my boots on the steps of the entrance and put down the stick by the side of the door. Once inside, I emptied the ruck-sack into the washing machine; while wandering over the mountains I had worn the same clothes over and over again for weeks, without any discomfort—but now that I was at home I smelled terrible. Later on while I was hang-ing out the washing, I encountered my neighbor the shep-herd, who had come to apologize for his calf. He was very sorry about what happened, and even wanted to buy a box of vegetables for me by way of compensation, but I thanked him and told him to forget about it. The vegetable garden had not been a good idea from the start. I was not sorry to see it revert to grass.

In front of the fire that evening I began to think again about the last few months. I contemplated the roof tiles, the outlines of wolves, bears, and owls in the knots and grain of the wood; I remembered the long spring, and I felt these things were as familiar as a childhood landscape. How many hours had this hut and I shared? I had run away from it pre-cisely because it knew me so well and had witnessed the angst-ridden moments of my solitude. Now I had returned, bruised and a little stupefied from my August wanderings as if from a nocturnal escapade. I felt that there in the hut I had no reason to be ashamed of myself. It welcomed me back and invited me to rest within its walls. Or perhaps it was only the autumn that was just beginning.

*　　*　　*

In the morning I went for a stroll in the woods. I found juniper berries and bilberries to add to my grappa. The undergrowth was now punctuated with thick, yellow larch saplings, some of them like drumsticks in the clearings, a few fly agaric toadstools; it was as if the mountain, after a long incubation, had finally entered into the harvest season. I sat down with my nose in the air, observing the canopies of the trees, the play of sunlight between the branches, thinking about Rigoni Stern's *Wild Arboretum*: I was living at higher altitude than he had done, up where there was no trace of beeches, ash, oaks, birches, the whole variety of trees that grew in the woods near to his home. At eight thousand feet there are only four types of trees, the only ones that can survive the mountain winters, and I felt a sort of devotion toward them—as if they were the protecting saints of this environment. So I decided to begin my notebook with an acknowledgment of gratitude to Fontane's little arboretum:

> I feel respect for the spruce, as for the inhabitant of a dark country. It lives on humid mountainsides and shaded valleys, where man does not build or cultivate the land. The humidity helps it to grow quickly: it has a light, spongy wood that's suitable for insulating houses from the cold.

My respect is a formal one—for a tree that I will never fully understand. I am troubled by its indifference to the changing seasons: an evergreen is like a face that never changes its expression. I am wary of its perfectly shaped foliage that makes it difficult to distinguish one specimen from another. The great swathes of spruce remind me of the forests of the North, of lakes, fjords, and snow. But one rainy August afternoon I took refuge beneath a spruce, and was grateful for that tree's dense needles and for the soft, dry carpet beneath it that provided me with a kind of den.

I admire the Scots pine as a type of pioneer. It is the first tall-growing tree to colonize areas of scree, the gorges swept by avalanches. The poor soil makes it a tree with an irregular and bizarre shape, each specimen different from the next, bent and contorted like the bones of elderly mountain folk. It is impossible to get from it wood for building with. It isn't even suitable for burning in the stove, because the fumes from its resin encrust the pipe and end up setting fire to it. But that same resin perfumes the wood awakening from its hibernation. That smell reminds me of the South and of the sea: perhaps because other pines perfume the air of the Mediterranean scrub. So the Scots pine is a dream of sunshine in the snow-covered wood.

I love the larch like a brother. The larch for me is the smell of home itself, and of the fire in its hearth. A line of larch trees is what I see when I raise my eyes from the sheet of paper and look outside. On windy days they sway like ears of wheat. The larch spends long months slumbering before putting forth its buds in April, then changes color with the advancing summer, from the intense green of June to the faded one of August, to the yellow and russet of October. It loves the sun, the southern slopes of mountains, dry soil, and wind. It seeks out the light, pushing itself upward above its neighbors: that's why the lower branches tend to dry up, as happens in life to things that we leave behind, and little effort is required then to break them and be free of them. But the fragility of the branches guarantees the solidity of the trunk: the timbers of the roofs of houses are made of larch. At the top the mountain folk customarily engrave the date of their construction: the most imposing houses of this valley go back to the beginning of the eighteenth century. While observing them I think of those venerable four-hundred-year-old larches, one still passed in the woods and the other three holding up a house—and it seems to me that this is the most noble service a tree can render to a man.

I worship the Swiss pine like a god. The stick with which I walk is made from it: it has a white wood that does not yellow with age, and is strong and supple in the races along paths. Elsewhere it is found in woods, around here instead it is a solitary tree that grows extremely slowly. It has seeds which birds conceal in their secret larders, in crevices in rocks at high altitude. Then a little soil and a vein of rainwater is all it takes: the last outcrops of pine grow up there, on the brink of precipices, on the crests. Sometimes they assume tortuous shapes due to the acrobatics they must perform in order to grow, due to the snow that twists and bends them, and the lightning that splits them. I have found the bravest of trees at eight thousand feet, a small Swiss pine that had grown on a ledge which protected it from the wind and collected a little water for it from the sky. It seemed to me as if I had discovered a secret temple, and I must have uttered before it something like a prayer.

Words

Remigio used to read all sorts of things—but mostly he read "difficult" books. That year it was Sartre, Camus, and Saramago. It was astonishing to be walking along a track and to hear these names, reflecting the contrasting nature of our trajectories as readers: I, the urban graduate, had ended up rejecting intellectual authors and falling in love with American narrative of the frontier and of the street; he, having grown up in a mountain village and not completed secondary school, was at the age of forty discovering the classics. He told me about his solitary childhood, that of a shy only child without friends. Very early on he had begun to work as a bricklayer with his father. He preferred work to school and had a reflective character, and at a certain point he became aware of a serious limitation: the words that he knew were not sufficient to express how he felt.

I stopped. We were walking in the wood at the end of August, coming across no one. What do you mean? I asked, intrigued. In the sense, Remigio explained, that he had always spoken in dialect, and the dialect had a rich and precise lexicon with which to designate places, tools, tasks, the parts of the house, animals, but was suddenly vague and imprecise when it came to feelings. Do you know what you say in dialect when you are feeling sad? he asked me. You say: *It seems long to me*. Which is to say, time does. It is the time that, when you are low, never seems to pass. But the expression is also appropriate for when you are suffering from nostalgia, when you feel lonely, and when you no longer like the life that you are leading. At a certain point Remigio had decided that a handful of words was not enough: he needed new ones to express how he felt, so he had set out to look for them in books. That was why he had become such a voracious reader. He was looking for the words that would allow him to speak about himself.

Like everyone up there, he had both a summer job and a winter one. In the summer he used to renovate old houses. In the winter he would drive a snowcat on the ski slopes. The shifts and the pay did not appeal to him at all, but the landscape did: at night, alone, with an immense white space around him, the spiers of rock at ten thousand feet lit up by the headlights, some music playing in the cabin—and outside the wind, or the thick fog, or the starlit sky.

Once he had almost lost his life. He was twenty-five and was working on one of the lower slopes—the one that passed nearby to my hut. At a certain point he had seen the larch trees bent down to the ground, and had time to be surprised by the force of the wind before the updraft of air had run over him as well. It wasn't wind, it was the front of an avalanche. The air had been sufficient to shatter the windshield. Remigio had come around after who knows how long, inside the wreckage of the snowcat, which had been crushed against some trees. He was hurting all over, but he had managed to extricate himself and to drag himself down to a lower altitude. He told me that his worst enemy during the descent had not been the pain but the fatigue, the temptation to stop and rest. And he had discovered a part of himself that was ferociously attached to life, and it was this that had brought him back home. Having reached it, he lost consciousness the moment that he crossed the threshold.

But he did not say *home*. Although he was obsessed with houses, when he had to refer to his own he resorted to circumlocutions. Let's go to my place, he would say. Or: to where I live. Not once did I hear him say: *to my home.*

I wondered why—I who after only a short time started to call home wherever I happened to be living. Perhaps it was because he did not feel at home anywhere, or because one house was as good as another since his home was the entire valley. I envied this about him: this belonging to a vaster place, to woods, to streams, to the shapes of mountains, to the piece of sky that the mountains framed, to the seasons that transition there.

Since he had never moved from his village, he fell in love with the people who came and went. It was something that had happened ever since he was a boy. It was with outsiders that he preferred to talk: like a stone that asks a bird what is on the other side of the mountain.

In return, when he made friends with someone he would take them to a special place, a big gloomy lake that resembled him—and it was there that we were heading that day. He pointed places out along the way, calling them by their names, but they were not villages or peaks marked on any official map: his map consisted of a wood, a clearing, a hole in the ground, a boulder plonked in the middle of a pasture. Do you know what this place is called? he would say to me. The *pian de sardognes*, the *pra' pera'*, the *sasc murel*, the *borna de' grai*. These place names did not appear in any land registry. Few remembered them now: they had defined borders and properties, but as soon as the mountain had been abandoned they'd fallen into oblivion. And so Remigio, who as a young man had delighted in new words, now mourned the passing of old ones, just as he did for the ruins we would come across as we climbed. In their time these houses had also been named. *Fontane, Champette, Brengatze, la Pelletzira*—each house had either a name which you could eventually see the point of, or one that was a memento of someone or something no longer remembered. Then the roof came down, the walls collapsed, and the last pieces to fall were precisely the names themselves: they would disappear one after another until nobody would know what that stone was called, that clearing, that ditch, and the mountain would have freed itself not only of mankind but also of its need to give names to things. Sometimes Remigio would remember a word but not its meaning—it was only a sound that he'd heard as a child—and then he would question his mother, who was eighty years old and had five cows and two dogs, and lived outside time along with forgotten words.

He guided me among the ruins like an archaeologist. He had spent a lifetime reconstructing houses, and had visited so many. In chests he had found documents three to four hundred years old: wills, deeds, building plans.

He explained that in the distant past, when a new house was commissioned no plans were drawn; it was enough to list the rooms it would have, as if from an imaginary catalog: a stable, a hayloft, a space for threshing rye, one for cheese making, balconies for drying hay. The ruins we visited were even more simple. Remigio would point out the details: the way in which a chimney had been built, or a niche in a wall, or the arches above the windows. It was from these particulars that the building could be dated. He would explain the techniques in minute detail while I paced impatiently in the doorway, because inside it was dark and outside the sun was shining, and I much preferred the meadows and woods to those piles of damp stones with their deathly atmosphere.

We had discovered that we enjoyed walking together. We would set out in the late afternoon, when the few remaining hikers were heading back down. We would race up for an hour or two, and at sunset the mountain was all ours. We would stop at the foot of some scree and come up with a new route every time. There was always a stream to retrace, or a track along a gorge. Shall we go up that way? one of us would ask. Then going up we would come across chamois that stared at us surprised, before vanishing with two or three bounds. And what are you doing here at this hour? they seemed to ask. Don't you have a home to go to?

Remigio would take photographs of them. This was something that remained of his father's "passion." They were herds made up of between fifteen and twenty individuals; the joy of our races culminated there, not at the summit crosses or among the tables of a refuge, but in the midst of rocks as the sun was going down, exchanging glances with chamois. We would like to have told them not to run away, since we were only passing through. The fear they had for us was the one insurmountable obstacle: we could bathe in a lake, feed on blackberries and bilberries, sleep in a meadow, but the wild animals took to their heels, reminding us that we were not and would never be one of them.

I felt better beneath the waterfalls or by the side of streams, near to running water; Remigio preferred the still. Furthermore, his lake was particularly gloomy. On one side the mountain had collapsed, and the scree reached down to the water's edge, forming a kind of cliff. On the other bank there was a slope which had been colonized by willows and rhododendrons, cut by a stream that surfaced a little farther above, and which fed the lake. Clinging at mid-height, where the slope softened into a pasture or two, some huts were still holding out. One of them belonged to Remigio. It had been built against the rock face, so that only three walls were needed instead of four, and it had natural shelter from the avalanches. He pointed it out to me from below, guiding me step by step with his index finger along an imaginary path. Eventually I thought I could make out something in front of a rock wall, the same color as the rock.

Can you see it? he asked.

Yes, I said, lying.

Would you like to go up and see?

Of course, I said, let's go up there.

A Visit to the Hut

In September someone came up to see how I was. We hadn't seen each other for some time. We spent two days together that seemed quite long, due to the degree of concentration they required of me. When he left, I picked up my notebook and wrote:

I've seen a hand and a foot belonging to my father sticking out from the sheets this morning. How strange it was to have him there, on my sofa bed, a guest in my home. My father is a man who has always slept little. Yet this morning on the floor there was an empty glass and yesterday's *Corriere*, its pages messed up, disordered like all newspapers that have been read from back to front. He must have been studying it the whole night through, drinking the Scotch whisky he'd brought for me before falling asleep when it was already getting light outside.

135

Due to the light that was filtering through the skylight he had pulled the sheets over his eyes, and this is how I found him.

How many other times had I seen my father in bed? The last time must have been a Sunday afternoon in Milan. When our arguments had woken him up he would summon me and my sister to his bedroom. In the darkness he would establish who the guilty party was, and would pronounce their name in a loud voice: the accused would tremble, the other was safe. He didn't even sleep later when I would get back at night and find him in the kitchen with his grappa and newspaper, and would have preferred him to say with words what he said with his eyes, so I'd have had the chance to reply: Listen, it's my life.

And it was still my life now, as was the sofa on which he was sleeping, the glass from which he had drunk, my father being nothing more than a guest in my house. His hand at sixty-four was the same as his hand at forty. Gnarled, dark, all knuckles, with the wedding ring that could no longer be slipped off its finger. The foot sticking out from beneath the sheet resembles the hand, except for the nail of the big toe which is thick and yellow, a bony nail broken during downhill races along mountain tracks. My father has never found the correct boot for his right foot. Among the songs he taught me, my favorite seemed to speak precisely about this. *With shoes or without shoes, I want my alpine troops beside me.* He had done his military service in the mountains, and when I was a child he would sing of the Great War. The stories of shoes, trains, sweethearts, and wine in those songs were a part of us.

So I imagined lifting the sheet and finding him like this: coal-black hair and beard, demonic gaze—and feeling those goose bumps again I put on the coffee and went out.

Outside I washed my face in the fountain and collected the bowl that the dogs had licked clean during the night. When I went back in, my father wasn't there.

Later, after he'd left, I found a larch tree up above in the woods which had been stripped bare by lightning, and to which a very strange thing had happened. A single branch near the base was still alive. The lightning strike had damaged the trunk but helped the branch, which had somehow changed direction, beginning to grow vertically and already forming almost another trunk. So there were currently two versions of that old larch: one that was charred and denuded, the other full of birds.

Due to what had happened in the last few days, I thought at first that the new trunk could be me, and the old one my father. But then it occurred to me instead that I might be both trunks, the old and the new, and that the lightning was really the thing that I had been waiting for, the fire that kills your old self so that the new one can emerge. In this case my father was just another tree in the wood. I turned around to face him, startled.

A Lucky Dog

I swear that if I am ever reborn I will come back as a dog, Gabriele said, watching the puppy he had adopted that summer being showered with kisses and hugs by every passing girl. Someone—not he—had named him Lucky. He had been born in the village from a border collie mother and an unknown father, and had been taken up to the alpeggio to learn from Lupo how to work as a sheepdog. But perhaps his fly-by-night father had bequeathed him a vocation along with his inverted colors: white with black markings, the lithe flanks of one born to run, the bell around his neck audible as he followed every walker that passed. Gabriele would shake his head as he watched him wandering off again. That dog had no interest whatsoever in cows, only in people. Sometimes the walker in question was me, and I would try to dissuade him: no, come on, don't follow me, stay with your owner! Lucky would wag his tail. If I scolded him and tried to escape, he took it for a game and would follow me even farther. I resigned myself to taking him with me, to test his mountaineering potential. To the best of my knowledge dogs are not natural climbers: he would clamber onto the crests and go fleet-footed along the ridges like a young chamois, and had nothing in common with those menacing guard dogs that in the pastures would growl at intruders. Where did you come from? I would ask him as he proudly heaved himself onto a rock to survey the valleys, adopting the pose of an ibex. Just having him around was enough to put me into a good mood. Down at Gabriele's there was a small chain hanging from the wall, and on my return, with a heavy heart, I would tie him there so that he wouldn't follow me home. Then Lucky would broadcast into the sky all his sorrow (Will you listen to that voice, Gabriele would say), while Lupo headed to faithfully guide the cows back into the stable, as if nothing else in the world interested him as much as that task. They were stepbrothers destined to hate each other, the only son and the adopted one, the stay-at-home and the nomad. I would cover my ears going down to Fontane, in order to avoid the sound of that howling.

Autumn announced its arrival with small signs, and not only with the darkness that seemed to fall a little earlier each night. It was there in the dew on the lawn in front of the house when I went out with my morning coffee. In the shadows of the larch trees that I saw lengthened at noon. In the wild animals that, once people had disappeared, started to show themselves again: the roe deer would come at sunset to graze the pastures, the fox would come closer in search of food. The wood vibrated with activity that I could glimpse when I went to cut firewood—the dart of a squirrel on a trunk, the leap of a hare in juniper, shadows moving. Mario Rigoni Stern used to say that of all the seasons the one he liked least was summer, because life hides itself from man as if it wasn't there at all—whereas he loved the autumn because it urges us to sharpen our sight, to open our ears and listen. But he did not speak of the somnolence that I felt enveloping the mountain. Of the dry riverbeds, the grass scorched by nightly frosts, the scents that each day faded a little more: no more hay, no more resin, no moss. In the air the smell of woodsmoke was beginning to spread, and that of the manure that the shepherds were spreading before leaving. After the nightly rain I was beginning to see snow whiten the mountain summits—then to appear lower at eighty-three hundred feet, eighty-two hundred, eighty-one hundred—only to melt again in the afternoon sun. With the thinning of the vegetation the sounds seemed to travel farther: so sometimes I would hear a tractor and then see it going along the road a mile away down in the valley. To the scream of the chainsaws in the distance was added the voices of the potato pickers bent double in vegetable allotments, extracting the fruits of the soil. Every evening, from above I would hear: Lucky! Lucky! And sometimes, but not always, the bell on his collar as he responded to the call.

Have you seen Lucky? Gabriele came to ask me. No, I hadn't seen him. He had been missing for a day, and we heard nothing more about him until the following one. Then someone called from the dog pound to say that he'd been found aboard a bus on the return route from school, after it had emptied of boys and girls and only the driver remained, some eighteen miles away from our place. Nobody had any idea as to how he came to be there, but no doubt his excursions had taken him even farther afield. Soon we discovered that he must have had a liking for the open road as well as for mountain paths, given that he would jump on board almost any form of transport that presented him with an open door. As soon as he became adept at this, Gabriele's number was circulated among all the kennels in the area, and along with the phone calls fines began to arrive.

The dog's a beatnik, I said.

What? he asked, hardly in a mood for literary references. He was angry, and understandably so: he had picked up Lucky as a working dog and now found himself obliged to pay for his excesses. The chain became habitual, as a form of punishment. I would pass by and see him chained up, half strangling himself to get free. I was allowed to free him in order to take him for a walk, but after the madly excited greeting, the race, the chasing after marmots, snapping the clip back onto his collar made me feel guiltier than ever.

Do you know anyone who's looking for a dog? Gabriele began to ask me, with a detachment intended to hide his sadness. He had fallen out of love with him, but not completely. I think he secretly liked the vagabond in him. Lucky, Lucky, he seemed to be thinking, we could have been friends you and I, as he gave him last melancholy caresses. Lupo would watch this scene from his corner with his snout on the ground, teeth half-bared, his annoyance barely concealed in a low, private snarl.

———————

I definitely did not want a dog; I had never wanted one. First, it would have prevented me from traveling. Second, it would have distracted me from writing. Third, fourth, and fifth, it would have deprived me of my freedom in ways that I could not even begin to imagine. And besides, how could I stomach being called its *owner*? So when I crossed the threshold of the hut with Lucky I was more preoccupied than happy. I thought that I would cook lunch, my way of becoming friends with the inhabitants of the mountain: I boiled water for enough pasta for two, but he was so famished that he ended up having mine as well. Having polished it off, he took possession of the shaded corner beneath the table. So I cut a piece of bread and cheese for myself, sat down at the table, and opened the notebook as I had started to like doing—scribbling a few notes while nibbling on something. With Lucky that habit of mine was short-lived. He smelled the toma cheese, got up, and came to rest his muzzle on my lap, drooling on my trouser leg. He ended up with the crust, and a little more besides. I had hardly put pen to paper before he was too bored to remain and headed toward the front door. He was staring at the door handle, looking at me, wagging his tail, then came back to the table to prompt me before returning to wait at the door again. The bell around his neck spoke eloquently of his restlessness.

We gotta go and never stop going till we get there, Neal Cassady would say to Jack Kerouac—and Lucky to me.

Where we going, man? we asked.

I don't know, but we gotta go.

I thought that the bell no longer had any use, so removed

it together with the leather collar to which it was attached, and hung the collar from a nail in the wall. This marks the end of your career as a sheepdog, Lucky, I told him. I thought he would have been pleased to no longer carry that reminder of his bondage, but he was indifferent to symbols and only interested in action. So it was that I finally opened the door and went out with him for a walk.

Desarpa

The last Saturday in September arrived, and from the freezing air that was blowing I sensed that I did not have many more left there. Climbing up the track I crossed a long line of slow-moving cows accompanied by dogs and young men making sure that none lagged and delayed, a man at the head of the procession and his wife at the rear, driving a tractor with a trailer full of stuff. It was the *desarpa*. The shepherds came down from the alpeggi, not because it was too cold but because the grass had run out. They descended silently, without needing to goad the animals or to speak among themselves, and I didn't know if what I was reading on their faces was fatigue or melancholy. One of them greeted me. Is that your dog? he asked. He follows me about, I replied, embarrassed, unable to say or to conceive that he was actually mine.

Having reached the top, we did a round of the now shut up alpeggi that until recently had resounded with the sound of cowbells. Lucky was sniffing out in one place and then another the life that had just left: doors and windows barred, the dunghill empty. The small channels that brought water from the streams to the drinking troughs and the stables were all dry now. Rusty overturned bathtubs had been left to languish in the pastures. On the ground there was dried manure, the tracks left by tractor tires, the stake to which the dog had been tied. They seemed like things that had been left behind in a hurried exodus, as if a war or an epidemic had broken out. Only the nettles were thriving, but those weeds grow well where there is no one left—they signal abandonment.

Climbing beyond the last pastures I jumped with one leap over the stream that in June I had removed my socks and shoes to ford: it had been reduced to a series of pools in which trapped trout stagnated. I could have caught them with my bare hands. The water in the lakes was leaden, almost black. A crust of frozen snow shrouded the north-facing banks. Lucky licked it, scratched it away with his teeth—something in him was made for the winter, and he sensed its approach with excitement. I was cut out for the summer instead, and was relieved on the run down to find myself once more treading on grass.

Reaching Gabriele's place I thought of my friend who was warming himself with his cup of coffee, alpine butter, sugar, and red wine—an infernal concoction which I had found myself having to drink out of politeness or in order to save face. I found him in front of the stable, with wedges and sledgehammer, splitting a stack of wood taller than he was. No longer having to pretend to be brothers, Lupo and Lucky were already open enemies: they circled each other with the hairs bristling on their backs, and then the older one flipped the younger, pinned him to the ground, and sank his teeth into his shoulder and thigh. Lucky yelped with pain and terror. Lupo! shouted Gabriele, flinging a block of wood in his direction so that Lucky was able to escape and limp toward the house, while Lupo sloped off, offended like someone prevented from merely acting within their rights. I gazed at Gabriele somewhat shaken by the violence of the scene. Dogs, he said, shrugging his shoulders. Soon I would get used to it as well.

The old larch tree must have grown twisted, and obstinately refused to become firewood: to split it you needed three or four wedges, and to expend a lot more effort than usual. Gabriele did not object to setting his tools down in order to get his breath back. When I asked him whether he was sad to see everyone leaving he feigned indifference, as if nothing would change for him when left up there alone again. As far as he was concerned, the desarpa was not something that he thought about at all; with a certain bravado he declared that it was only a question of supplies: with a full cellar he could hold on up there until Christmas. But I could see from his eyes—from the way they avoided mine—that this was only a pose, and that in reality the autumn would weigh heavily on him as well.

What day is it, Saturday? he asked. How about it, shall we go into town and have a skinful?

I replied in the negative, withdrawing from my role as drinking companion. I knew that I was disappointing him, but the last time that I'd "had a skinful" it had taken me two days to recover, and the drinking bout in prospect promised to be a sad and nasty one.

I found Lucky on the balcony of the hut, licking his wounds. He had a puncture wound in his thigh that was bleeding. That will teach you to keep your distance, I said to him. Autumn is a cruel season, and it makes us cruel too.

The next day my neighbors also left. I felt sorrier that the dogs were going than the men, with whom I'd never managed to connect. I would miss the sound of the bells that announced their visit. Since Mozzo arrived walking, Billy at a trot, and Lampo at a gallop, I had learned to identify them by the different sounds they made. They left without any farewell visit, and I thought that was for the best. It's well known that dogs do not like partings, and such rituals are not to my liking either. It was like another piece of the summer gone, withered, superseded; when nothing at all was left of it I would be ready to close the door and leave.

But Mozzo, Billy, and Lampo were replaced by other dogs, and they were not accompanied by a lively tinkling of bells. One morning in October I was woken up by their barking. I looked out from the doorway, holding Lucky so that he would not dart out to join the fracas, and I saw a pack of hounds running back and forth from the wood, heeding the calls of two strangers. The strangers had binoculars around their necks, shotguns slung over their shoulders, and were wearing camouflage fatigues. It had not occurred to me that one of these days the hunting season would begin. The dogs ran around hysterically, excited by the scent of prey: from that morning onward the scene repeated itself daily, and shots began to reverberate in the hours before dawn. Then Lucky would go into hiding under the bed, and I pleaded with the god of the wood that those shots would all be wide of their mark. I was thinking about the roe deer, the chamois, the stags that were so prized. During the week, at sunset, the turning place at the end of the road became a gathering place for hunters: the deer would break cover at that time to graze the edges of the pastures where the fertilized grass is lusher than in the clearing. With their binoculars the hunters monitored their movements for six days. They counted them, measured them, even selected them; they seemed to be saying: that one's mine, I'll take it, keep your own hands off it. The deer did not know that the seventh day would be fatal, that they should have observed the Sabbath and stayed in hiding.

There was an old hunter who passed by the hut every morning. He would operate only in the woods nearby, perhaps because he simply couldn't cover any more ground than this. One day I heard two shots and shortly afterward I saw him leave with a hare hanging at his side from its back legs, its long gray ears reaching to the ground. I felt instinctively that this was my friend: the hare whose footprints I had caught sight of in the spring, when I was afflicted by loneliness and my encounter with it had meant so much to me. The same hare that every evening would study me from a distance, making me hope that sooner or later, with the force of habit, it would find the courage to come closer. Now I felt ashamed of having domesticated it even to this extent: I had set a trap for it, for how could it distinguish between me and the man with the gun? Its death seemed like an intolerable crime to me, and I hated that old man with all my heart.

In the Whiteness

Yesterday, in the afternoon, it started to snow again. Dry, floury, winter snow that the wind whipped into spirals everywhere, and that collected on the threshold of the house and on the pile of firewood stacked against the wall.

So what is this, October? I thought.

Not even the larch trees had had a chance yet to drop their needles. Their branches drooped low and would sometimes suddenly snap. I no longer heard the bellowing of the stag, or the shouts of the hunters.

During the evening I stayed by the window, reading and gazing outside. The snowflakes were illuminated by the light from the house. I was reading a book by Sylvain Tesson, *The Consolations of the Forest*. Lake Baikal, cigars, vodka, thoughts of a far-off brother.

It was still snowing, and I had just begun to cook supper when the gas in the tank ran out. The blue flame turned yellow, then flickered and was gone. Goodbye soup, I thought.

I wrapped four potatoes in silver foil and shoved them into the embers in the stove, and an hour later I ate them, crisped and scorched, dipping them into salt, washing them down with red wine.

It must have been around nine when the light also deserted me. The lamp above the table went off. The song on the radio was cut short halfway through. The fridge abruptly ceased buzzing.

The whole house was plunged into darkness and silence, apart from the crackling of the fire and the sound of the mouse that had been running around in the kitchen cupboard for the past two days. Outside, the snow fell soundlessly.

I resigned myself to the situation. What else could I do?

I unfolded the sofa bed, prepared it in the firelight cast by the stove, fed and stoked the fire, and got under the covers. The sound of the fire in the dark was good company.

After a few minutes I heard the dog, who had moved from his place under the table to get onto the bed, trying to do so without making a sound, as if he could join me there without being noticed. He curled up at the bottom of the bed, and I placed my feet snugly beneath him.

During the night I must have dreamed of writing a story about a man who runs out of everything—gas, light, pen, and paper, as his life is suddenly reduced to the most elementary state—while above and all around me it snowed and snowed.

That morning the world was a blank page.

The sky was clear, with a blue made more intense in contrast with the snow-covered woods.

I went for a look around to see how much snow had fallen, and sank down to my knees in it as soon as I'd gotten beyond the front door.

Lucky was in his element: he went ahead of me in bounds; he dived, filled his mouth with it, rolled around in the fresh snow. Maybe you were a sled dog in a previous life, I told him—you're not a car thief, you're a prospector for gold.

The larch trees freed themselves at the first sign of the sun, sloughing their loads—and beneath they were green and yellow.

*   *   *

Because I liked the trees, the snow, and the sky, if I'd had a camera I would have framed my pictures portrait rather than landscape. There is something solemn about a snow-covered larch in morning light. I thought of Pavese: "For my part I believe that a tree, a stone silhouetted against the sky were gods from the very beginning."

At home I scraped the ice off some wood, lit the fire, then remembered that I'd run out of gas. The electricity had not returned. So I made coffee in the embers, Turkish style, blackening the bottom of the small saucepan in the process.

When I sat down at the table my notebook was there waiting for me—stopped yesterday, stopped years ago, on that very line, at the exact point where I had left it just before it started to snow.

A Last Drink

"The end is important in everything," says the *Hagakure* of Yamamoto Tsunetomo, and I spent the last day up there thinking about this, that I wanted it to end well. In the morning Lucky would wake me up by licking my face, and we would go to check on what the ice had done: I would snap off the long stalactite of ice that hung from the fountain, would clench it in my hand until it stuck to my skin, then let it float and melt among the larch needles that had fallen into the water. If it had been a clear night the thermometer would show five below (about 20° Fahrenheit). I would light the stove, prepare the coffee, follow the tracks left by the mouse who was keeping me company. During the night it had explored the bench in the kitchen, the rings on the cooker, the basin, circling the shelf where the pasta and rice were stored, digging between the floorboards to extract crumbs of bread. I no longer knew what to do with him: at first he had been shy, venturing out only in the middle of the night. Then he had understood that he was tolerated by the master of this house, and he had begun to take liberties, so that now I sometimes saw him even when I was cooking. We can't go on like this, I would say to myself, as I cleaned up the evidence of his activity throughout the hut. I should have accessed the rough mountain man in me, picked up the broom, and exterminated him. I had just recently broken my walking stick while crossing a stream. Its metal tip had got stuck between two boulders, and as I pulled to release it there was a sharp *crack*. I had decided not to look for a new one, since I would have no use for it. But I had kept the pieces of the old one: this Swiss stone pine, peeled with Opinel and dried in the sun, scratched by the stones of scree slopes and polished with sweat, this companion of many adventures throughout that long summer, would end up in the fireplace on the last night. And perhaps afterward I would stop getting attached to mice, sticks, and the shoes on my feet that were falling to pieces.

Gabriele continued to maintain that he would go down when his wine ran out. Very amusing, but I had learned to recognize his jokes. The demijohns had been empty for some time already, and we had been reduced to buying boxes of wine from the supermarket. The truth was, that without consulting each other, the three of us—Gabriele,

Remigio, and me—had all decided to leave at the end of October. There was snow on the way, the real kind this time. So one of us had found a room to rent in the village, and was emptying it of its old furniture in order to install a stove, a cot, and a table; another would move to his winter home, even if he would never call it *home* either; and I would go back to the city, to looking at the mountains from a car window, while in traffic on the Ghisolfa Bridge. But first I had a last project to realize. For a long time I had wanted to spend an evening with both of them, but they were both quick to evade my invitations. Despite knowing each other forever they had for some reason never become friends, and this saddened me given how attached I was to both of them. One day in October I tackled this head-on and said, Listen, I'm cooking tonight so bring something to drink and no excuses—think of the evening as your present to me. And they really did make a gift of it. Slightly embarrassed, both in their best clothes and each carrying a bottle of wine, they presented themselves at my door just as it was getting dark. "In the house I had three chairs," wrote Thoreau, "the first for solitude, the second for friendship, the third for society." I was just in time to experience this myself, in our little mountain community. If I achieved anything worthwhile up there, if I had to choose one thing of which I am proud, it would be that I managed to get my friends to sit at the same table, and enjoyed my time with them before leaving.

I spent the last day preparing the hut for the winter. In the vegetable garden overrun with weeds I scattered the ash from the fireplace. It probably wasn't much good as fertilizer, but it seemed like a fitting thing to do. It was like picking up the larch that had fallen in the spring and returning it to the mountain. With a few shovelfuls of soil I filled the hole in the ground where I used to light my fire outdoors, and stacked the remaining wood under the balcony. I brought in the saw, scythe, spade, and rake. Then I washed my hands in the ice-cold fountain and gave a last look around. The place was once again as I'd found it—only Lucky, who had not been there then, stared at me without understanding. Are you ready for the city, I asked him, you unfortunate creature? In his life to date he had yet to lay eyes on a leash or pavement. We're going to have to cure each other, you and me, I told him. Perhaps you'll teach me how to make my escape with the aid of the first car that passes.

At lunchtime Gabriele arrived and said: I'm not very good with goodbyes. Neither am I, I replied. Well then, goodbye, he said. He no longer had the huts; he was working on the ski lifts. They were dismantling the seats, oiling the gears, and tightening the bolts in anticipation of the coming ski season. He moved away on his tractor, with Lupo biting the front wheels as he always did, barking and getting in the way—as if to say stop, where are you going, go back. Instead Remigio threw me out of the house when I went around to say goodbye, pretending that he had important things to do, then shortly after, writing a message to apologize because he was sad and had not been able to give me a farewell embrace. I understood well enough.

I had not been up to the mountain for a while; in the morning it was covered in a crust of ice. So I took advantage of that sunny afternoon and set off with Lucky immediately after lunch, climbing quickly because I knew that I had only a few hours left before dark. Then it was like crossing the finishing line and keeping the tape. Reaching the ridge and discovering again, after so many months, an unknown aspect of it, taking a route I'd never taken before. Then going down the other side and reaching a meadow burned by ice. Peering through a window in an alpeggio now closed for the winter, the plates shelved with the jars of conserves, the look of someone having just tidied up before leaving. Studying the mountain and choosing a beautiful line to take—beautiful for those who know the beauty of going where there is no path, crossing high up on the routes of the chamois. To go beyond the abandoned burrows, the split tree trunks, the larches burned by the fall, crossing scree by leaping from boulder to boulder among the bare rhododendrons. Bathing your face and hands in a stream. Tasting the October bilberries, the plants now divested of foliage but still heavy with fruit as sweet as raisins, dark and shriveled after nights of frost.

I used to do this as a child—one last look around to say farewell to the mountain. I would write some notes and hide them in broken rocks, in the split bark of trees, so that my words would still be there after I'd gone.

Now we must go, I said to Lucky. It was time to go back down. I already knew all the dreams that I would have that winter.

About the Author

Paolo Cognetti was born in Milan in 1978 and is a graduate of the Civic School of Cinema in Milan. A passionate reader of American literature, especially short stories, he has published two short story collections, *Manuale per ragazze di successo* (*Manual for Successful Girls* [2004]), *Una piccola che sta per esplodere* (*A Small Thing About to Explode* [2007]), and a book of linked stories, *Sofia si veste sempre di nero* (*Sophia Always Dresses in Black* [2012]). Since 2004 he has spent several months a year in New York, his spiritual heartland, where he developed his feature-length film *The Wrong Side of the Bridge*, a journey among his favorite Brooklyn authors. In 2010 he published with Laterza the nonfiction work *New York e una finestra senza tende* (*New York Is a Window without Curtains*), followed by *Tutte le mie preghiere guardano verso ovest* (*All of My Prayers Face West* [2014]). He is also the editor of the anthology *New York Stories* (Einaudi,

2015). He divides his time between the city and his cabin six thousand feet up in the Italian Alps, and loves to travel.

His first novel, *The Eight Mountains* (Einaudi, 2018), won the Strega Prize in Italy and is currently being translated into thirty-nine languages. He has written a great deal about the places to which he has traveled. His latest passion is for Nepal, about which has written in *Senza mai arrivare in cima* (Without Ever Reaching the Summit [Einaudi, 2017]). In 2017 he established with some friends a festival of art, books, and music in Estoul, in Valle d'Aosta, where he lives for six months of the year. He also intends to open a mountain refuge as a site for cultural activities and artists' residencies.